Table of Contents

Dedication

To the pioneering women, past and present, that I have had the honor to know and work with.

Genevieve sat at her writing desk staring at the snow being lashed by the winter winds outside her window. Her bag was packed for the trip, waiting downstairs by the front door of her uncle-in-law's rambling Victorian home in Denver. She pulled the shawl close, scrunching her shoulders to the shiver of anticipation and the unknown awaiting her. This would be the culmination of all she'd worked for these many years since she and her mother-in-law moved from the East coast to live with her brother. Shortly thereafter, she took on a position of director of a mission sponsored by the congregation of the Denver Methodist church—the church where her step-uncle served as deacon board member and his wife played organ. Her position was as a matchmaker of sorts, director of the Benevolent Society of Lost Lambs. Fairly new to the church, the group had been a place to house women who found themselves in circumstances unknown, needing assistance. They welcomed all women of various age, races and family dynamics. With the onset of the many catalogs that popped up and the advertisements soliciting brides for the men who'd gone west in search of making gold and land claims, Genevieve became aware that these seasoned women (some more than others) deserved a happy marriage and if there was any possibility of a new chance for some of these women the Society of Lost Lambs was the hope for many.

The soft glow of the kerosene lamp cast shadows on the bundled stack of letters sitting never far from reach on her writing desk. The blue ribbon faded and frayed now with time served as a reminder of why she'd chosen the path of match-making. She picked up the pencil and began the entry on the blank page of the journal her mother-in-law gifted her on this new adventure.

December 1876

Tomorrow we board a train bound for the first leg of our trip to Noelle, Colorado. A small, but picturesque little town (if Pastor Hammonds description holds true) blossoming ripe for new families. The women I travel with are a diverse lot yet among us is a camaraderie, a purpose—a hope. Our common desire is to establish hearth and home in this New West. These are not your delicate flowers of society. For the most part, they are seasoned (some more than others) resilient, capable women who I am certain will be an asset to the admirable suitors Pastor Hammond has so carefully chosen. The way is paved with uncertainty. Most grand adventures are. And I will be there—at their side—not only as a representative of our society's goals, but also as a woman, making sure that each of these women I have come to know receives the happiness they so richly deserve...

Genevieve paused. Her gaze lighting on the intricate patterns of frost on the window pane. Would there be houses such as this? Draped canopy beds with thick quilts piled high for warmth on a winter's night? Warm wool-tufted rugs underfoot? The scent of a warm stew wafting from a well-stocked kitchen? She had her doubts that Noelle was Utopia. She glanced at the letters and the gold watch on its delicate gold chain.

Time.

The war had taught her the meaning of it. A short-lived marriage. A widow's mourning dress. A forbidden kiss from a man deemed her husband's closest confidant—she shook her head to dissolve the ancient history. A dozen years had passed. There'd been no word after his departure. It was better left as it was, she had finally convinced herself. She had a new life. A new mission. Genevieve picked up her pencil and with a cleansing sigh finished the first of many entries to come—

"I retire now with a sincere hope during this season of miracles that our journey together makes us stronger, and that the camaraderie we share through common experience will be a bright and shining example of our mission purpose. May our God go with us and may He bless these women with long and happy marriages."

Genevieve picked up the letters and tucked them in the tapestry satchel she'd carry with her on the train. The watch was placed with her other dressings laid out and ready for the early morning train.

Chapter One

The eleventh day of Christmas
January 4, 1877
Noelle, Colorado

Genevieve dabbed her eyes with the lace-edged handkerchief given to her as a wedding gift by her mother-in-law. Bittersweet memories lodged free from her surrounding stung as sharp as the wintry Colorado wind.

Her wedding day. That, too, had been a winter's day, a lifetime ago—the intimate gathering, the house aglow with festive warmth. Thoughts of war had been set aside at least for a few hours. The images blurred, but the emotions attached to them--long since thought buried--surfaced with stark clarity at the sight before her.

A small tree, gaily decorated. A potbelly stove providing warmth against a cold, bitter wind. A bride, holding a simple nosegay of evergreen and ribbon awaiting her marriage vows. A handful of women who'd been virtual strangers but a few days ago stood together on this frigid Wednesday morning, bonded by the journey that had brought them from Denver to Noelle, Colorado—their future home.

Genevieve glanced at the watch—her husband's—that had been returned to her after his death.

A quarter past the hour and Penny's intended, Silas Powell, appeared to be late for his own wedding.

Birdie Peregrine looked at Pastor Hammond. "Shall I send Jack to look for him?" she asked, her blue eyes sparkling with determination.

The preacher smiled amiably. "Thank you, Mrs. Peregrine, but I don't think that will be necessary. Silas isn't exactly known for his punctuality. Let's give him a few more minutes."

Birdie shot a questioning look to Genevieve. After all, she was the matchmaker that had managed for the most part to marry off a number of the brides she'd escorted from the Benevolent Society of Lost Lambs in Denver, just ten days ago. She nodded. "The pastor is right, let's wait a few moments more." She forced herself to smile at Penny whose stoic gaze unsettled Genevieve.

Birdie patted Penny's shoulder, then fluffed the lacy veil the gifted seamstress had made for the new bride. Birdie had taken a particular shine to

Penny over the past few days after news began to circulate through town that this was Penny's third trip to the altar, due to the untimely deaths of her previous husbands.

Genevieve had found the woman's penchant for ill-fated luck remarkable, but chose instead to see it as merely coincidence. However, considering the strange incidents revolving around Penny over the past couple of days, convincing miners--already a superstitious lot—had not been so easy. Even Silas, her intended, had gone out of his way to avoid his prospective bride after the debacle of spilling his whiskey on her barely after they'd arrived. And their arrival in the midst of a snowstorm on Christmas Eve was nothing that any of them had expected.

Genevieve caught Pastor Hammonds ever-present smile. She'd come to realize that most times he used it to elicit a calm assurance. Today, however, it served as a reminder of the struggles and hardships that lay before these women in this barely civilized place. A place she had thought this side of heaven given Pastor Hammond's poetic portrayal of an idyllic place to establish a home and family for each of her prospective brides.

Not all had wanted to make the journey despite the pastor's rosy description. Penelope Hamilton Jackson was one such woman. She'd come to Denver after hearing of the society's benevolent work and had offered her services to help other women. It had been Genevieve who had talked her into giving married life one more chance. Begrudgingly, she'd agreed, and Genevieve had her twelve brides she'd promised to escort personally to Noelle. True, she could just as easily have sent them off on their own. There was nothing in the agreement stating her presence was necessary on the journey. To accompany them had been her choice and one she'd not taken lightly. She felt wholly responsible not only for their safety, but also to verify the men chosen were acceptable companions for marriage. In addition, she wanted to prove to her superiors that the mission could be useful in placing a variety of diverse women in good marriages.

Pastor Hammond held her gaze as he spoke to the small waiting crowd. "Folks, I like to think that God performs some of his best work in times like these. Let us raise our voices in song to pass the time."

His voice, a rich baritone began, "God rest ye, merry gentlemen…"

Those present, mumbled along, appearing less certain it appeared that music was going to change the current course of things.

Genevieve stared at the preacher. He'd offered the same congenial smile as they stood ankle-deep in the drifts during a blinding snowstorm. Emerging weary and frazzled each woman shivered beneath the only capes they had over their thin dresses. The narrow passage through the mountain pass would have been harrowing enough in decent weather, but the storm created its own dangers and she'd been grateful the wagons were covered so that the women couldn't see how treacherously close to the edge of the mountainside they were at times.

Half-frozen and scared, they looked to her, uncertainty glazing their eyes. Genevieve had taken one look at the less-than-picturesque surroundings and turned her gaze on the good preacher for a clear explanation. Climbing down from the make-shift sleighs (crude wooden wagons modified with runners) to the snow-crusted street she and the other brides took in the tumble-down buildings, most in need of repair, they followed Pastor Hammond into a building with Golden Nugget saloon painted across the upper half of the structure. Genevieve's heart wondering of the nightmare she'd shepherded these women into.

She'd not been moved then by the Pastor's charming smile. Indeed, she'd been livid to discover that they'd been brought here under a delusion that Noelle was like heaven on earth. She'd threatened to return to Denver post-haste if the pastor didn't secure a suitable dwelling for the ladies until each was married. Herded in to the saloon, they'd waited and watched as a handful of men determined a solution to the problem.

"There's only one place big enough and nice enough for those lasses." Genevieve overheard the saloon's bartender speaking aloud.

It was the pastor who had encouraged Sherriff Draven- a man who appeared fresh off a wanted poster—and through negotiations she'd preferred directly not to be part of—to be in charge of letting a woman named Madame Bonheur know that her ladies would need to relinquish their home called for the new brides at La Maison des Chats, which according to discussion was one of the most lavishly furnished buildings in Noelle—at least until all the brides were wed.

Arguably, after seeing the rest of the town, it was the most habitable of all the structures in town, but the take-over had not endeared Madame to Genevieve nor her brides. Especially since it meant that madam and her resident ladies had been forced to move their business across the street to an abandoned two-story ramshackle saloon.

That had been eleven days ago. At present, it seemed like an eternity.

Genevieve sighed. After a week of watching her brides married off she realized that Pastor Hammond was not the only one guilty of having created a façade. She, too, had embellished on the truth. In her correspondence she'd painted glowing profiles of each woman in a glorious light. Descriptions that any sane man would kill to marry. In truth, this odd mix of women was a broad study in diversity and eccentric backgrounds. Each came from tumultuous lives, seeking a fresh start in a new place. And with any luck, she hoped to deliver to each woman the happiness they truly deserved.

But with each passing day she'd come to realize that, as rough as it appeared, Noelle had promise. She felt confident that the women she'd brought to this little town had the potential to create a solid, close-knit community. Aside from that, the railroad hierarchy hadn't given them much time to create a plan for survival. Desperate times called for desperate measures. The town needed brides to secure its survival and she meant to see to it that they met that need.

"Ack! What *eejit* brought in that godfersakin' goose!" Seamus, the Golden Nugget bartender, chased the squawking bird from behind the bar, swatting at it with a hand towel.

Molly Thornton lunged for the goose as it waddled through the small group of women, nipping excitedly at their skirts.

Pastor Hammond paused only a heartbeat before he raised his chin and sang a little louder over the din. A cacophony of honks, song, and shrieks filled the room. Genevieve stood to one side taking in the scene, wondering seriously about God's sense of humor.

"Storm, you and yer missus best be gettin' this varmint out of my saloon or it'll be gracin' my dinner table this very night!" Seamus threatened.

The quiet man rose calmly from his chair, working with his new bride to try to capture the belligerent fowl. They cornered it finally behind the festive little Christmas tree that had been set up near the front window of the saloon. Seamus, known as a lovable curmudgeon with an Irish temper, had at first, thought it a bit too prissy for a saloon, but had gotten into the spirit of things with everyone involved. However, by the eleventh day, the bartender's patience had worn thin, and so too, his pockets, complaining the saloon was losing revenue. He was more than ready to get back to the daily task of pouring whiskey and breaking up bar fights.

"Pastor Hammond," Seamus growled in agitation.

The preacher ceased his singing and looked at the ruffled barkeep. "I agreed on a daybreak wedding only because Mr. Hardt is my boss and he owns this saloon. But *I* run the place." Seamus glanced sheepishly at the waiting bride. "You may recall we open early on Wednesday for cards and beer." He glanced out the dingy thick-paned windows then back at the preacher. "I got men waiting outside and the wind is as cold as a witches ti--" He swallowed the rest of the statement realizing the curious gaze of several female eyes were upon him.

Pastor Hammond raked a hand through his thick hair and spoke with strained patience to the man "Well, then Seamus, why don't you have the men step inside. They can wait there on the other side of the room for a bit," he reasoned. "It shouldn't be too much longer."

Genevieve glanced around at the handful who'd come to witness the wedding at the crack of dawn on this winter morning. Most of them the brides previously married-Meizhen; wife of the official animal expert in town--Woody Burnside, Birdie; wife of Jack Peregrine of Peregrines Post & Freight, Fina; wife of diner owner, Nacho Villianueva, Kezia; wife of the blacksmith, Culver Daniels and lastly, Molly Thornton; recently married to Storm who crouched on the other side of the tree cornering her frightened pet goose, and of course, Felicity, the Reverend's new wife. Along with that sat a handful of motley-looking miners who'd been released from their duties for the day by mine owner, Charlie Hardt in order to celebrate Silas's marriage.

Not exactly the celebration Genevieve had had planned.

Stomping across the room in a huff, Seamus opened the door and once more the gusty winds assaulted them. He impatiently ushered the half-frozen men inside. The group ambled inside, stamping their boots, slapping their arms and eyeing the warm wood stove on the other side of the room. All avoided eye contact with the waiting bride. As instructed, they huddled around a table shoved to the side of the room, a few finding chairs. Most leaned against the wall, arms folded across their chests, dubious of the whole thing.

All at once the tree shook with a life of its own. It's branches, laden with select ornaments denoting each Noelle marriage thus far, bobbed and swayed precariously as the goose made known his displeasure at being imprisoned behind the tree.

"Don't go scaring him, Storm," Molly admonished her new husband. "He's bound to have a fit if we don't calm him down."

With a sigh and wondering how much more chaos God truly needed to perform His miracles, Genevieve rose to see if she could lend a hand at capturing the goose.

A thud outside stopped her in her tracks as the door flew open. A fierce winter gust grabbed the door and sent it back against the log hewn wall with a loud bang.

Reacting on instinct, several of the men had drawn their guns and had them pointed towards the man, his face partially hidden by his wool neck scarf. He raised his hand in the air. "Pff-astor," came a muffled voice. Seeing the guns pointed in his direction, the man removed the scarf.

Chapter Two

Zeke brushed the skiff of snow from his brother's tombstone. Heating the harmonica with his breath, he put it to his lips, and tried to get through a stanza of "Amazing Grace" on the early dawn of this frigid January morning.

It'd been three years since Clem's death. An accident at the mine had claimed his life. Damn fool. It'd taken Zeke and several men to clear the rock that had buried him. All those years Zeke had survived the war, glad that his brother had been safe at home on the farm. He'd agreed to come west after the war to support his baby brother's pie-in-the-sky dream of claiming his gold strike and making it rich. More than anything he'd come to watch out for him.

Damn lot of good that had done

A lump clogged Zeke's throat. He tucked the harmonica—his constant companion during the war--back in his coat. He only played it now when he came to visit Clem.

He blew out a frosty breath and straightened, gazing out over the spot where several markers dotted the landscape. Some had been killed by hostile Indians, some by harsh winters, others by disease, and the quest for gold had taken its share. He glanced down at the marker, still unable to purge himself entirely of the guilt.

The pounding of horse hooves on the frozen ground brought his head up. A lone figure on a horse broke the early morning shadows, it's rider headed north toward the mountains. It was rare to see anyone out on this edge of town before dawn and that's precisely why Zeke chose this time to visit Clem's grave--for the solitude. He didn't care much for small talk or talking in public. People always have a lot of questions. The folks in Noelle had finally accepted that about him. They lived their lives here. He lived his in the mountains. It worked out.

The rider slowed and Zeke recognized Silas Powell, foreman to Hardt's miners. Zeke nodded in greeting as the man tugged on his horse's reins. The mare appeared skittish, nervously pawing and prancing about.

"Headed up north to find work. This ain't the only gold mine in these parts. Don't supposin' you'd be interested? I could use a man with your Indian skills. I'd pay you handsomely when I make my claim. What do you say, Kyi-yee?" He narrowed his gaze on Zeke.

Zeke shook his head. There were times he rarely remembered his real name. Everyone from the elders of the small Ute tribe to the townspeople in Noelle called him by the name that meant *"the bear."* "As tempting as the offer is, no thank you. Gold no longer serves any interest I have in this life or after."

Silas huffed. "Suit yerself. I'm giving you fair warning, bad luck has come to this town." He pointed a finger at Clem's tombstone. "And I don't plan to stay around and end up like your poor brother."

Zeke eyed him sharply. He'd seen greed in a man's eyes before. He'd also seen its consequences. In a gesture he felt only fit, he pulled the leather necklace from his shirt. It had been strung by the Ute elder who saved his life from the bear attack that nearly killed him. It had since, served to protect Zeke. But Silas, on his journey would need all the help he could get. That and a word of caution was all he had to give to the man. "Take this. It might be helpful in trade if you encounter unfriendly Indians. Anything else and I'm afraid you're on your own, Silas." Zeke gave the man little chance of lasting the week in this rugged country. There was still much unrest between the white man and certain Indian tribes. Many tribes were being forced from their land in search of the elusive gold the government wanted/needed to replenish its reserves after the war that had depleted most of the country. If irate Indians didn't get Silas, then there was a good chance that marauders would. Thieves and scavengers were always on the hunt for guns, gold, horses-- whatever they could find from an unsuspecting rider.

Silas grabbed the necklace, tossed it over his head, and hastily adjusted his hat. "Much obliged. Good luck to you and take my word. You'd be better off making plans to head back east." He dug his heels into the horse's sides and off he flew like the devil himself was on his tail.

Zeke's gaze followed the man until he rode from sight. He shook his head. He hoped Silas made it to his destination, but in truth, his odds weren't good.

With a sigh, Zeke picked up the reins of the horse. "Come on, Blue," he said pulling his flatbed sled he'd built to transport his fur pelts. It had been weeks since he'd made a trip down the mountain. The better part of that time he'd been in the high country hunting a bear that had attacked the goat of one of the Ute tribe elders. With a short break in the weather, he'd decided it was an opportune time to bring in his pelts and trade with the local business folk to lay in supplies for the harsh winter months ahead.

The town seemed eerily quiet, even for dawn. He paused. Not even the constant sound of the stamping mill—known as the "drum" echoed out over the town this morning. Odd. Zeke glanced around, glad that perhaps the bitter wind had kept people inside today. He shrugged and pulled out a list of his chores in town written on a piece of yellowed paper and the stub of the only pencil he owned. He checked the short list of supplies he needed—flour, sugar, a bag of oats-he traded pelts for goat's milk from the tribe elder, but would need a new can of kerosene and a box of matches as well. Trudging up the ice and snow-covered street toward Culver's Livery, he hoped his friend wouldn't mind housing his sled of pelts in the stable while he did his errands in town. He made a mental note to speak too, with Woody about a runt donkey he'd talked into buying last spring. The little animal made a nice company, but lately hadn't been eating well and Woody was hands down the best source of animal care in the area.

He glanced up at the barber's sign and ran a hand down his long beard. It was matted and tangled. In dire need of a trim, he knew. Being back in civilization made him aware of what a sight he must be. Then again, at present he had no plans to prolong his stay in town.

He led the horse around the curve of the livery, reaching the stables just as Woody ran past him with nary a glance. Zeke searched further up the road expecting to see a cougar or bear causing the man to run like his tail was on fire. Whatever the cause, Woody--one hand planted atop his hat to keep it on-- was in one heck of a hurry.

"Morning, Woody," Zeke called, raising his hand in greeting. "Just going to get Blue some oats…if that's okay with you." Woody didn't slow. "Woody!"

With a quick glance over his shoulder, Woody kept right on running. "Help yourself. Be back in a bit. Got pressing matters here."

Zeke stared perplexed after the funny man--heart as big as the sky and there was no one he trusted more with his animals--but the man could be a bit *tetched* in the head at times.

He led the horse to the barn, lifted off the harness, and tied him in front of one of the watering troughs. Placing a bucket of oats in front of the animal, he patted its back, and grabbed one of the bundles of fox and deer pelts, tossing it over his shoulder as he lumbered back to the blacksmith shop. His bow knife, one given to him by his father, was in need of a good sharpening. The sound of clanking metal being hammered welcomed him as he came around the corner of the blacksmith's shop. The sound echoed in the still-silent street. Zeke glanced down the street, but Woody was nowhere to be seen. This had been one damn strange morning.

"Mornin,' Culver," Zeke said tossing the stack of pelts over a split fence rail. "Town sure seems quiet this morning. Where is everyone?"

The large man swiped his sweaty brow with his forearm. His undershirt was covered in soot and grime. He scratched his cheek with his thumb as he gazed down the empty main street. "Just saw Woody headed to the saloon. It's Wednesday. 'Spect that's where most folks are. Mine's closed for the day due to--"

Zeke's gaze followed Culver's as he turned to greet the statuesque woman who had come from inside Culver's quarters behind his shop. Her dark wavy hair was tossed over one shoulder, her dark eyes smiling as she carried a cup of steaming coffee to Culver. The scent made Zeke's mouth water. "Ma'am," Zeke said, nodding politely. He didn't recall ever seeing the woman before in town.

"Oh, Kyi-yee, this here is Kezia. My wife," Culver's chest puffed out a bit, his smile adoring.

"Wife?" Zeke blinked, taken aback, unsure he'd heard the big man right.

"And a new papa, as well." Culver took the cup, his gaze glued to the lovely woman.

"What?" Zeke said, unable to hide his surprise. "Did you say…*father*?" *Had it been that long since he'd spoken to Culver?*

Culver's expression clouded. "My Kezia has a six-month-old babe." He frowned. "You don't think I'm fit to be a father?"

Zeke put up his hands in defense. "No, no…I'm just…so happy for you, my friend." Zeke glanced around and wondered what else had changed in town. "When was this happy occasion—the wedding, I mean?"

Culver's surprised look turned contemplative. "Guess it's been nine days now." He winked at his new wife. "Yessir. Been nine whole days. Can't say it's been too bad, neither."

The woman looked at the ground where her leather slippers peeked out from beneath the gown. A heavy blanket covered her from head-to-foot. She offered a shy smile, speaking quietly. "I just came to tell you the baby is sleeping."

"Is she now?" Culver raised his brows and then grinned.

Rather than risk life and limb by asking more questions-in particular about the child—Zeke pulled out his knife from his tooled leather holster. "Uh, I just wondered if I might leave you my bow knife. It needs a good sharpening." Zeke wasn't at all sure that his friend heard him. "I uh, brought you some pelts. Thought maybe we could do a trade."

Culver put one arm around the woman's shoulders and started back to his room. Using his free hand, he pointed at a nearby table. "Leave the knife and the pelts there. I should have them ready in…say, an hour?"

"Sounds fine." Zeke couldn't wait to move on to his next chore.

"Make that two," Culver called after him.

Zeke cast a look to the sky and raised his hand, trying to ignore the fact that he actually thought he heard his big friend giggling.

First Silas's strange departure, then Woody, now Culver. What the hell was going on in Noelle? He fished out the letter he'd written to his parents and noticed the light on in the window of Peregrine's Post and Freight. He stepped inside and as always was in awe of Jack Peregrine's cabinet-making talents with his polished wood counter, shelves, and display cases. He had a deep regard for the skills of both Jack and his grandfather, Augustus—known by Gus to most of the townsfolk. Self-taught Gus had honed his craft in creating exquisitely detailed leather works. Having been close to his grandfather back home, Zeke had been immediately drawn to Gus when he and his brother had arrived in Noelle. Their mutual interest in learning their craft made them fast friends. Gus often bought Zeke's animal skins for his projects and Zeke, in return used to sit with Gus in the evenings and show him the art of whittling, as Zeke's grandfather had taught him. Since the mine accident and the events thereafter Zeke had spent little time in Noelle. Only coming down off the mountain when it was necessary.

It was quiet—almost too quiet. He glanced around. There was something different about the place. Zeke's gaze followed the wall behind the gleaming wood counter, similar to the one at the Nugget—which also was Jack's handiwork. His brows rose as he realized a newly finished shelf behind the counter. Stacked on the shelves were rolls of fabrics—bright, flowered prints, plain muslin, even lace—a very feminine addition to be sure. On the lower shelf were boxes offering buttons, needles, and trim. He looked around to make sure he was in the same store.

"What can I do for you, young fella?" Gus popped up from behind the counter, startling Zeke. "You'll have to speak up as my hearing ain't what it used to be." The old man studied Zeke and snapped his fingers. "Yer that

Kyi-yee, fella." He nodded as though affirming his comment.

"Got a letter here I need to send back home," Zeke said, pulling out the envelope from inside his jacket.

"Well, now." Gus held out his hand and Zeke handed over the letter. The older man squinted to read the address on the envelope. "All the way back to Virginny?" He frowned trying to read Zeke's penmanship.

"My folks are still on the family farm, sir," Zeke said.

"'Spect that's a mite difficult with you being all the way out here. Got any brothers helping out back home?"

The question was an unexpected punch to Zeke's gut. Had that accident slipped Gus's mind? Everyone in town had known about it.

"My...um, brother. He died here in Noelle a few years back. Mining accident, remember?"

The old man's eyes widened in shock, then he seemed to return to the present. "I'm sorry, son. My condolences. My memory ain't what it used to be."

"It's okay, Gus," Zeke said, eyeing the man whose stories he'd once spent many an evening listening to his colorful stories and learning about how Gus taught himself leather tooling. It was as though Gus hadn't recognized him at first, nor seemed to remember that he and his brother had stopped by often to send letters back home when they'd first come to Noelle. Zeke hadn't written for quite some time. His family knew of Clem's death, of course. But Zeke's guilt and then the long recovery from the bear attack had kept him from writing this letter—long overdue.

Gus's behavior only added to the strange goings on in town. From the moment he'd run into Silas nothing seemed what it used to be. It set his emotions on edge, bringing to mind the Great White Owl he'd seen last night as he carried in wood for the fire. Once dismissive of the great bird, he'd learned from the Ute elder who had saved his life that to the Indian, the bird signified a great change, an eminent storm on its way. Perhaps Silas had been right when he mentioned bad luck had come to Noelle? Something for certain brew on the horizon, he could feel it. Zeke cleared his throat. "You'll send it for me, then?"

"Oh, certainly. Certainly." Gus tapped the letter against the counter. "It'll only take a few weeks to get there by rail. Fastest thing I've ever seen."

"Fine, how much will that be?"

The corner of Gus's mouth lifted in a grin. "Say, you got any foxtails with you today?"

Zeke smiled. "Indeed, I do. My sled is over at Culver's Livery. I'll go fetch one for you."

Gus held up his hand. "Before you leave town is fine, son." He leaned forward slipping off his favorite cap. "Thought it might spruce up this cap of mine."

Zeke grinned imagining how a foxtail would look hanging from the old wool cap Gus had worn as long as Zeke had known the old man. "Well, to be sure the right tail can look mighty fetching on the right hat." Zeke glanced around the store. "Say, does Jack happen to be around?"

Gus snorted. "Third time this week *Sunny Boy's* been late for work." He gave Zeke a wicked smile. "I suspect he's worn out."

Zeke offered a curious look. "Worn out? Why's that?"

Gus looked around to make sure there was no one in earshot. "It's that new wife of his."

Another single man in Noelle married? "Wife?"

Gus frowned. "You gone deaf boy? You ought to have Doc Deane check them ears."

"No," Zeke said shaking his head. "I mean, when did he get married?"

"Oh, guess it's been about a week…yes, about a week." He grinned. "I've not seen Sunny Boy so pleasant in a long while. Does my heart good. Even heard him whistling in the backroom the other day." Gus leaned his elbow on the counter. "His Birdie is a pretty little thing, but, mind you, tough as nails. A hard-worker, that one. Cookin' ain't bad. A whiz with sewing 'n making things with her hands. I can see why he chose her to marry." Gus offered a lop-sided smile. "That, 'n he feels he needs someone to help look after me. But he don't know I'm on to him." Gus winked. "But I got a couple of things he don't know, too." He lowered his voice and offered an ornery grin. "Like I got me a lady friend."

Zeke grinned, imagining the man-about-town Gus might have been in his earlier days. "Do tell."

Gus leaned closer. "Well, only if you promise not to say anything just yet. I want to tell Jack myself." He waggled his bushy brows. "I been whittling her these little animals." The corner of his mouth lifted in a smile. "She's right taken with my talents."

Zeke nodded. Could this day get any stranger?

A loud squawking split the early morning quiet. Zeke and Gus stepped outside the store in search of the sound. "Is it coming from the mine?" Zeke asked.

"Appears that durn goose is creatin' havoc again." Gus let out a laugh and slapped his knee.

Woody had his chickens and they'd been known to create a ruckus now and again, but he didn't know anyone who had a goose. He caught the sight of a man and a woman running around the side of the Nugget saloon in heated pursuit of a frightened bird. He narrowed his gaze, not trusting his sight. "Is that Storm Thornton?"

"Heeheehee," Gus cackled. "That's the most excitement gone on around here in days." Gus glanced at Zeke. "Meaning outside of the bedroom, that is."

Zeke raised his brows at the old man's comment. A woman's voice screaming someone's name pulled Zeke's attention back to the trio. The feathered one was heading straight for the Cayuga River that ran along the back of the businesses to the north of town.

"I'm guessing his new wife's pet goose got away from her again," Gus said, chuckling. "She brings that varmint with her everywhere she goes."

Zeke held up his hand, unsure he'd heard the old man right. Storm Thornton wasn't the marrying kind. They'd had many a conversation over the very topic. "You mean to tell me that Storm got *married*?" Zeke sputtered. What the hell was going on in Noelle? Wait…maybe he was dreaming, or maybe this wasn't really the sleepy little town of Noelle?

Zeke looked at the old man. "It seems to me that while I was gone hunting these past few weeks, our little town has gone to hell in a handbasket."

Gus raised his shaggy brows and looked at Zeke. "Well, then son. You probably haven't heard about that matchmaker gal who brought all those women to town the other day. Arrived on Christmas Eve. Since then, the single men in town been droppin' like flies. You best be watching yer back." He grinned.

"Matchmaker?" The word put a bitter taste in his mouth. He'd had his own nightmarish experience with arranged marriages. The death of his brother, followed by an attack by a four-hundred-pound grizzly had convinced Zeke that perhaps there was more to life. He had once believed that settling down, raising a family was what he needed to quell the numbing loneliness he carried inside.

In a vulnerable moment, he'd read an advertisement in the Noelle paper about young women seeking suitable companionship for purpose of marriage. Although there'd only ever been one woman he'd given his heart to--and out of common decency he'd left before his emotions could outweigh his reason. She'd remained in his heart--the elusive love that could never be his.

Perhaps hoping to quell his loneliness, to start fresh with a new wife, he'd debated long and hard before deciding to answer her ad and give a mail-order marriage a try. In time, there was the chance he'd come to love her as she might come to love him. Gathering his meager savings, he'd sent her the money to travel west.

She'd arrived at the rail station in the town where the line stopped eight miles from the mountain pass into Noelle. She'd batted her pale blue eyes and offered a smile somewhere between seduction and innocence implying the promise of a future together. They made a beeline from the station to the judge in town, and Zeke had spared no expense in getting a room for their wedding night, promising the road back through the mountain pass to Noelle was far easier and lovelier by day. He'd thought naively that a few scars from his attack would not affect his new bride. He was virile, stable, young, and strong. But what should have been a blissful wedding night was short-lived when, after he'd removed his shirt, his new bride screamed, horrified by the welted scars of the bear attack across his shoulders and back. She'd insisted he sleep elsewhere and by the next morning he'd returned her to the train before it departed. Weeks later, he received a note that the marriage had been annulled.

"A matchmaker in Noelle," Zeke grumbled. "Now, don't that just beat all."

Gus smiled. "It's a shame you weren't here when they drew straws, young fella."

Zeke chuckled and shook his head. "Oh, no thank you." It was the first time that day that Zeke had been grateful for his extended hunting trip. "You make sure my letter gets mailed, Gus." He shook the man's hand and strode back to the stable, bent on fetching his horse and pelts. The sooner he got his tasks completed the sooner he could retreat to the peace and quiet of his home in the hills. Taking a glance down main street, he noted the large hand painted letters of the Golden Nugget Saloon. Zeke decided he needed a drink.

Chapter Three

"Woody?" Genevieve stared at the man as he pulled the scarf from around his neck.

His face was pale, his expression looking as though he might be sick.

"Woody, would you please shut the durn door, you *eejit*," cried Seamus.

All at once there was a flurry from behind the tree. Frightened by the bartender's angry admonition, the goose with a strangled honk broke free, causing the tree to list as it scurried, wings flapping wildly out the open door.

"Daniel!" Molly screamed and grabbed her skirts in pursuit of the fowl. Storm caught the tree, righting it, then raced out the door after his new bride. Despite their many differences, it was ironically his willingness to care for Molly's pet goose that most endeared him to his new bride.

Startled, Woody leapt aside as the bird and his owners disappeared in a chaotic sprint around the side of the saloon.

"What is it, man?" Pastor Hammond asked, trying not to let the agitation edge into his voice. He was a patient man, or so it appeared, but even his patience had been stretched this morning. The deadline of the contract made with the railroad hung in the balance, only hours away. Noelle's survival depended on there being no other catastrophes.

Brought to his senses, Woody pushed against the fierce wind and managed to close the door. He leaned against it, panting to catch his breath.

One final bob of a tree branch caused an ornament—a silver pipe made of painted glass to roll off the branch and shatter on the rough wood floor. It broke with a pathetic tinkling sound.

Genevieve's heart sank as she noted it was the smoking pipe ornament marking Penny's wedding to Silas.

Woody's terrified gaze flickered from Penny to the preacher and back to Genevieve. He swallowed hard. "Got some bad news, preacher. Silas Powell took one of the horses from the livery. Saw him just a while ago riding up the street. I was tending the mules when I saw him. I yelled for him to stop, but he didn't hear me." Woody's gaze went to Penny's. "I'm sorry, ma'am. But I thought you should know."

Pastor Hammond flashed a look at Genevieve. She saw his silent plea to assist in this awkward dilemma. Genevieve met Penny's unwavering look.

"Told me bad luck has come to town. Mines dryin' up," said one of the men who had worked alongside Silas. He glanced at the stoic bride.

"Heard him talking about it last night."

The jilted woman lifted her chin and Genevieve saw her struggle for control.

"I can round up some of the men and go find him, Pastor Hammond, if you want me to." Woody Burnside, as far as Genevieve could tell, was as earnest and helpful as they came. "He couldn't have gotten far."

"No," Penny said emphatically. She paused seeming to regain her composure. "No, thank you, Mr. Burnside. That is most kind, but not necessary." She looked at Pastor Hammond. "Very well, then, I think we're done here." She glanced at Genevieve, then pulled off the veil and handed it back to Birdie. "I won't be needing this."

Genevieve reached out to touch the woman's shoulder. She backed away. "I'm so sorry, Penelope."

She squeezed her eyes shut. "No need. I shouldn't have agreed to this. We both knew it."

Genevieve shook her head. "No, that's not true. This isn't about you, it's about Silas and…his greed." Genevieve looked over at the group of rugged men standing and joking about what had just happened. "Surely, there are men left here in Noelle." She raised her voice to be heard clearly from across the room. "Good, decent men, who by now have seen the improvement marriage can make in a man's life and have changed their mind. Why, any one of these fine gents would be honored to take Silas's place. Isn't that so, gentlemen?" Genevieve turned then and eyed the stunned faces staring back at her.

They held her gaze but for a moment before all of them rushed for the door like a herd of elk being chased by a mountain lion. They fell over each other to get out the door.

Genevieve pondered whether to follow them and keep walking until she made it back to Denver. "We can fix this, Penny."

The woman left at the alter opened her mouth to speak, but Pastor Hammond intervened. "Ladies, it has been a trying morning. Why don't you take Miss Penelope back to the house and fix her a nice cup of tea? I need to speak with Mrs. Walters."

"It doesn't matter," Penny said over her shoulder.

"I swear to you, Penny that by days end you shall be a bride," Genevieve called after the departing group. She collapsed at the nearest table, her head propped on her hand.

"I must find her a husband," she said, trying not to let despair filter into her thoughts. "She is wonderful, warm, and bright. She has so much to offer the right man. It's *finding* the right man that has been most difficult for her. I so want to help her find happiness."

Pastor Hammond sat down beside her. "Here. This will help...some." He handed her a small glass half full of amber liquid.

"I don't drink." She gently pushed it away. "Thank you," she added as an afterthought.

The preacher slid it back in front of her. "I didn't either. Trust me. One glass has an interesting way of putting life in perspective. It's only when you hit four or five that you care less about perspective. At that point, you're just trying to forget."

Genevieve eyed the glass, then tilted it to her lips and took a sip. Her eyes watered, her lips burned. It felt like liquid fire sliding down her throat. She covered her mouth as she fell into a fit of coughing.

Pastor Hammond patted her back. "I'm not sure that we can force anyone into marriage if they aren't willing."

Genevieve frowned. "Did you see how those men ran over each other as though I was asking them to give up an appendage?" She sighed. "Ten brides, Pastor Hammond--you and Felicity, Culver and Kezia, Woody and Meizhen, Jack and Birdie," she said, holding up a finger for each couple. "Draven and Pearl—and trust me, I wondered about those two. Storm and Molly—yet another questionable match. Liam and Avis, Cara and Dr. Colin, and then there's Nacho and Fina, and Hugh and Minnie—all complicated stories to be sure—but turning out happily for all involved." She sighed. "Ten weddings and only two more to go." She glanced at the pastor. "I had such high hopes for Penelope, in particular."

"There, there, Mrs. Walters. Perhaps this is all a misunderstanding. People come and go frequently in Noelle." He punctuated his comment with a heavy sigh. "Perhaps Silas will have a change of heart," he said.

"Or he'll run into hostile Indians and get his just rewards," she muttered. Eyeing her glass, she took another drink, longer this time, glad for the way it seemed to warm her blood. "I'm sorry, that's not a kind thing to say. At any rate, I doubt Penelope would be convinced to take him back were he to change his mind."

"Yes, and well...there is that matter of turning the other cheek," the pastor said, before sampling his own drink.

She pointed her finger at him. "What we need is to convince the single men left that there is nothing at all to these silly superstitions that Penelope in some way carries an aura of bad luck around her." She paused. "And you're just the man to do it, preacher," she said, poking his shoulder.

He looked at her, his expression skeptical. He shook his head. "I'm not sure we have that much time, Mrs. Walters."

Not to be defeated just yet, she tossed back the remainder of her drink. This time the burn felt good going down. The pastor had been right. Her perspective was actually becoming clearer. "Well, it seems to me if you can't convince them, then we must find a man who is not privy to the backgrounds of the women I've brought from Denver. Someone who has not been swayed by the rumor mill." She smiled and lifted her glass. It was a superb idea, really, if she did say so herself. "I find this drink quite amiable once you get used to it. What is it, exactly?"

Pastor Hammond smiled and Genevieve returned it. God was lucky to have a man so charming on His side.

"Well, in times like these I always remember the assurance that God gives us in Matthew 19:26…with God all things are possible."

"Ah." Genevieve pointed her glass at him. "But in your case, sir, time is of the essence. Let's hope that Noelle has had enough chaos today to warrant God's attention."

Pastor Hammond smiled. "Don't lose heart, Mrs. Walters. I firmly believe that when God closes one door, He opens another."

The saloon door opened and, with a rush of wind, blew in what appeared to be a large, rather deformed grizzly bear carrying a belted stack of fur pelts over one shoulder.

Genevieve's eyes widened as the fur-laden creature strode in, slamming the door with such force that the remaining ornaments on the tree quaked in the aftermath. Mud and debris left a trail behind the fur boots wrapped snugly around his calves. Her gaze crept slowly upward taking in the muscular thighs covered in doeskin trousers, every firm muscle showing beneath the tight covering as he moved.

Genevieve licked her lips, blinking two or three times to make sure that her sight was not influenced by drink.

He wore a jacket made from what appeared to be a heavy blanket, tethered around his waist, giving greater definition to his broad shoulders. On the belt hung an intricately tooled leather holder, presumably for a large knife that would usually lie against his hip. Perched atop a mass of dark, straw-colored, shoulder-length hair he wore a hood, fashioned from the head and shoulders of a bear. A scraggly beard and moustache covered most of his face.

He tossed the pelts onto the sleek polished mahogany bar and pushed back the ghastly looking hood from his head.

"Them things better not have claws that scratch that wood," Seamus warned as he approached the man with a bottle and glass in hand. "Mr. Hardt wouldn't take kindly to his bar getting roughed up."

The man glanced at Seamus without expression. "Hardt can come see me if he has an issue," he said quietly.

Seamus raised his brows. "Just trying to keep things peaceful, Kyi-yee."

He poured a drink and set it on the counter.

"Who…or what…is that?" Genevieve leaned over and whispered to the pastor.

"He is our resident hermit. Goes by the name, Kyi-yee. It means "bear", so I'm told. The name was given to him by the Ute tribe that he trades with. Most of the Indians have been peaceful to deal with, others not so much. It has been beneficial to have him around when tensions arise. He lives alone somewhere up in the mountains."

"Does he have a Christian name?" she asked, unable to keep from staring at the way the doeskin stretched over his backside when he leaned forward against the bar. She swallowed hard, her throat suddenly dry.

"I'm sure he does. But he was here before I came to Noelle. That is what the townsfolk call him."

The man hadn't acknowledged their presence. Instead, he tipped back his head and, in one swallow, emptied the glass.

"Was that what we drank?" she asked in whispered awe.

Preacher leaned close. "That's Seamus's special hooch. Well over one hundred-proof, I understand. Kicks like a mule."

"He doesn't seem at all affected," she marveled.

Pastor Hammond seemed to do a double-take. "Mrs. Walters, whatever is going on in that lovely head of yours, I think it best to let it go," the preacher admonished.

Seamus turned to leave, bottle in hand. The large man reached out without looking up and snatched the bartender's arm.

"As agreed. Five pelts for a bottle," he said in a low-timbered voice that sent a shiver skirting down Genevieve's spine and, lord help her…lower.

Seamus scowled, nodded, and left the bottle. He grabbed the pelts, eyeing them briefly before carrying them through the curtain to the backroom.

The man straightened his shoulders, raked a hand through his unkempt long hair, and poured himself another drink--downing it as quickly as the first. He certainly appeared healthy—exceptional physical health from her observation. Genevieve was surprised by her visceral reaction to the stranger. It had been ages since a man had affected her in such a way. Perhaps it was the alcohol that led her to see his stellar qualities of a desirable companion—self-sufficient, fearless, ruggedly handsome. Probably, beneath all that hair. "I would imagine he is also good with his hands," she said, more to herself. Upon seeing the pastor's shocked expression, she realized she'd uttered the words out loud. "Meaning, he's likely a carpenter as well. Perhaps grows his own food."

Pastor Hammond raised an impervious brow. "Of course, I thought that's what you meant." He turned his face, but not before she saw him grin.

"The truth is, he likely knows nothing about any of the brides or their backgrounds." She narrowed her gaze, attempting to determine his age—around mid-thirties, she estimated. "This hermit—this mountain man, as you call him--surely, he could use a woman in his life, don't you think?"

Pastor Hammond shook his head. "No, ma'am," he said quietly, and turned to face her. "I don't think that is a good idea."

The man downed a third glass and Genevieve wondered if he was thirsty or trying to forget—and, if the latter, what could it be?

He wiped the back of his hand over his mouth and only then seemed aware there were others in the saloon.

Genevieve was astounded by the fact that she'd been in Noelle all week and had not in all the men she'd encountered found such a fine specimen of rugged male in all the men she'd encountered as this one.

Penelope. This is for Penelope.

The man glanced from the preacher to her, holding her gaze a bit longer--perhaps her imagination—before offering a neighborly nod and turning away.

Duty and determination laced liberally with liquid courage, edged its way into her conscience. She thought of Penelope, of the agreement to save

Noelle. And, more importantly, if this venture proved successful, how well it would bode for her and the mission's future.

Pastor Hammond leaned forward and spoke in a whisper. "I don't care for that look in your eye, Mrs. Walters. I'm certain there has to be another way."

Genevieve met his gaze. "I'm not so certain that we have a choice. You're out of straws and the clock is ticking, Pastor Hammond. Do you wish to save Noelle, or not?"

All at once, the fur-covered man flipped the ghastly hood over his head and strode toward the door, with his gaze unwavering. It was clear he was not interested in being social.

That, however, did not deter Genevieve. This was for Penelope. "Excuse me, sir?" she called to his departing form.

The beast of a man hesitated at the door.

"Oh, lord," she heard Pastor Hammond mutter.

Genevieve swallowed. She hoped that, living alone somewhere in the woods, living off nuts, berries, and God knows what—that he was still somewhat able to carry on a civil conversation. Nonetheless, she was glad for Pastor Hammond's presence. "I wonder if Pastor Hammond and I might have a few moments of your time?" She glanced at the pastor who appeared less enthusiastic about the prospect.

"You are familiar with our good Pastor Hammond?" she asked primly folding her hands.

"I am," he replied, still facing the door.

"Would you be so kind as to please look at me when I address you?"

He straightened then, his height made all the more intimidating by the bear turning to face her. She met the glassy, dark eyes of the bear first and, lowering her gaze, looked directly into the bluest eyes she'd ever seen.

Her heart stopped. Twelve years had passed since she'd seen such blue-eyed clarity. But of course, that was only a coincidence. She blinked to clear her muddled thoughts. "My name is Mrs. Genevieve Walters." She cleared her throat, perplexed by the man's penetrating gaze. "I-I have brought twelve women to Noelle under contract with your mayor and Pastor Hammond--"

Pastor Hammond lifted his hand with a brief smile.

Difficult as it was to get past the eerie memory the strange man's eye color evoked, she forged ahead. This was about Penny, not ghosts of

Genevieve's past. This was about saving Noelle, not some stolen kiss—now ancient history--nor the man who'd stolen her heart, then left without goodbye. This was about proving herself an exemplary matchmaker. "Mr. Kyi-Yee, we have a proposition to discuss with you. Something that will benefit not only you, but Noelle as well."

"No."

Genevieve was taken aback, in part by the voice that skated over her, but more by the fact that he hadn't even heard what she had to say. "Why, sir, you haven't yet heard our proposal."

The man glanced at the pastor. "Does it have to do with marriage?"

Pastor Hammond lifted his shoulders and nodded.

"Not interested."

"But, Mr. Kyi-Yee--" Genevieve insisted. Good lord, if ever there was a man in need of a wife it was this one.

He opened the door, setting the Christmas tree branches to sway, the ornaments to bobble precariously yet again. The silver pipe still lay in tiny pieces on the floor. Genevieve rose to follow the man.

Pastor Hammond grabbed her hand. "Mrs. Walters, I implore you. Think of Miss Penelope."

"I am," she said, pulling her hand away. She tugged her shawl around her, greeted by a bitter wind. The sky looked dank and cloudy as though it might snow.

Squinting against the icy air, she needed only to search for a bear walking on hind legs--and that went double for his personality. She spotted him, his stride long and determined, heading down the street.

Remembering her vow to bring happiness to Penny's life she set out to follow him, picking her way down the street over the icy slush and snow.

Chapter Four

"Pardon, amigo, but I could not help but notice the nice matchmaker lady over there. She has been looking at you." Nacho, owner of the small diner in town, set a steaming plate of *huevos rancheros* in front of Zeke.

"I hadn't noticed," Zeke lied. "You have any more coffee, Nacho?" he asked, purposely avoiding the woman's gaze and his friend's curiosity. He attacked his breakfast as though it was his last meal. And it might well be if the new matchmaker in town discovered his true identity. But that wasn't going to happen.

"Did you hear the news that Silas Powell left town?" Nacho topped off Zeke's mug with more of the rich coffee. "My Fina, she said that he left his bride waiting this morning at the altar."

"Fina? Who's Fina?" Zeke eyed the man. He firmly set his fork down. "Oh, no. Not you, too?" he asked. "Is *everybody* in the damn town married?"

Nacho shrugged. "Not those who didn't volunteer to draw straws, no. And of course, those that were not lucky to be chosen as grooms." He grinned.

"Straws?" Zeke asked. "How long?"

"Have we been married? Just the past two days."

"And how's it going so far?" Zeke was being polite. He really had little interest in marriage. But the matchmaker? He couldn't deny the punch to his solar-plexus when he'd turned around and came face-to-face again with Genevieve Walters. It was as though she'd been able to reach in and pull his heart out of his chest with just one look. He pulled himself back from his reverie just as the man finished his impassioned narrative of his wedded bliss.

Zeke shook off the cold dread in his gut and smiled at Nacho. "Well, then congratulations." Zeke gripped his friend's hand. "Is there anyone else I know that is recently wed?"

Nacho seemed to ponder the thought. "Storm Thornton. He married Miss Molly. Culver, he married Kezia…oh, and Jack Peregrine married Miss Birdie. Then there's Woody--"

Zeke held up his hand. It was just as the matchmaker had said. She'd brought twelve brides to town to marry twelve of Noelle's men.

"Nacho, why now? What's the big hurry to marry?" He'd know this man ever since he and his brother came to Noelle.

Nacho slid into the chair across from Zeke. "Marriage. Family. It suits me. I believe man was meant to have a companion, no?"

Zeke raised his coffee mug. "Spoken like a true Christian." Raised in the Methodist church, Zeke had probably believed the same, once upon a time. But seeing brother against brother, the hatred, the bigotry and sorrow of the war had left its mark on his beliefs—a scar on his very soul.

"A wife is a good thing," Nacho admonished with a smile. "My Fina brings new light to my life."

Zeke leaned back in his chair and listened. He scratched his cheek and studied Nacho. "That's mighty interesting and noble, my friend. Why is there suddenly such an all-fire hurry to get everyone married?"

"Oh," Nacho smiled. "Of course, it probably seems strange to come back to town after a time and find many of the men married."

"It is a might unsettling," Zeke agreed.

"The way Pastor Hammond explained it was that he--"

"Decided we needed to get some of the men married?" Zeke asked.

"No. It's my understanding they came up with a plan to save Noelle."

"Didn't realize Noelle was in need of saving." Zeke listened carefully.

"Everyone knows the rumors that the mine is going dry. That is why so have many left—hearing of the strikes out in California," Nacho said. "But Mayor Hardt doesn't believe the mine is dry. He's got Hugh Montgomery testing the rock."

"Spring would be a better time for that. When the run-off is fresh and washed down from the mountain," Zeke said, thinking aloud his thoughts.

Nacho nodded. "*Si*, but Mr. Hardt is not the type of man to give up so easily. If they can come through with the deal they made with the rail line, then perhaps it will give the mayor more time to find what he's looking for, no?"

"What kind of *deal*?" Zeke questioned with a frown.

"If Noelle can prove it is a thriving community—that people are willing to raise their families here--the railroad will consider bringing the line on through Noelle."

Nacho's sea-green eyes fairly sparkled with glee. "Think of it, Zeke. The train making a stop right here in our little town."

"And that's why the men volunteered?"

Nacho nodded as he stood. "I need to get back to work. Fina is cooking today. It's probably best I don't leave her in the kitchen alone for very long."

Zeke eyed his friend carefully. "So how many are left to be married?"

Nacho thought. "Just one if Silas hadn't taken off. Now there's two left. Miss Penny and Miss Agatha--though I heard rumor she hasn't yet found a man in Noelle deserving of her skills.

Zeke raised a brow. It dawned on him then what *proposal* Mrs. Walters was so hell-bent on offering. She needed a stand-in groom for--

"Who was the gal Silas stood up?" Zeke asked his friend.

"Miss Penny," Nacho answered. He picked up a stack of dirty dishes, balancing them on his forearm. He paused at the table. "It is perhaps only rumor, but it may be that Silas feared for his safety."

"His safety?" What kind of brides had been brought to Noelle?

"She is a widow woman—twice. There seems to be something odd about her. There are those who are superstitious and claim she is bad luck."

"Well, then maybe Silas did the right thing by leaving. Though I'm not sure riding out there alone is any better an option as far as luck goes. He might have fared better taking his chance with Miss Penny."

Nacho nodded in agreement. "I will say a prayer for his safety." He turned to leave and, in doing so, opened up the view of Mrs. Walters seated across the room. She had a determined look in her eye.

"Oh, Nacho?" Zeke said, waving the man back to his table. "Be sure to tell your new cook these eggs were mighty fine."

Nacho grinned. "*Bueno. Gracias.* She will be pleased to hear this."

The sound of someone choking across the room captured Nacho's attention. "I told her too not many chili peppers in the sauce." Nacho glanced at Zeke. "I must go, *mi amigo.* Say, perhaps you should speak to the matchmaker lady about a bride, no?"

Zeke chuckled and wiped his mouth with a napkin. "Oh no, thank you. I'm fine with my life the way it is." He waved Nacho closer. "But to ensure my unmarried status, would you do me a big favor?"

"Of course, Kyi-yee. You only have to ask," Nacho replied.

"Go over and keep the matchmaker busy. I need a head start." Zeke grinned. Though the idea of having Genevieve Walters chasing after him had a certain appeal, her reason for doing so was not personal—it was business. Fact was, she needed someone to marry "Bad Luck Penny," and he had no intention of marrying her--or anyone else, for that matter. In fact, he had no desire to face Genevieve Walters after all these years. He'd wondered what had happened to her. How she managed. Whether she and her mother-in-law had moved to Denver. But every time he picked up a pencil to write, he feared taking her from the safety of her family bringing her out here where nothing was certain and life was difficult, if not dangerous. No, she was better off where she was and while it took a long time to quell the desire thinking of her conjured inside, he dove into his work and tried to forget.

"*Gracias, mi amigo,*" Zeke said and hurried out the door.

Thanks to Nacho, he was able to escape before Mrs. Walters could get to him. Chances were good that he'd only bought a little time before she caught up to him.

Walking towards the barber's, he stepped off the diner's flat wooden porch and nearly ran into his friend, Storm Thornton coming around the corner.

"Storm," Zeke greeted the man while eyeing his somber expression. "You catch that goose of yours?" Zeke held back a blurt of laughter. His friend shook his head and sighed.

Zeke had known the man and his grandfather, Ezra for a number of years. Storm had left the mine to pursue other interests after surviving the accident that had killed Clem, Zeke's brother. Guilt over his brothers accident had pushed Zeke into his self-imposed exile into the mountains that nearly cost him his life.

"Yes. We finally got Daniel back home. Molly wanted him to be at the wedding. He's…very special to her." Storm shook his head. "You do understand it was my grandfather who volunteered me for marriage."

Zeke looked over his friend's shoulder so he could keep an eye on the door of the diner. He raised a brow, offering a grimace. "No, I didn't realize." He studied the man who looked wearier than he remembered. Then again, one might reason that newlyweds would naturally appear fatigued given the new marital responsibilities…. Zeke cleared his throat, dispelling thoughts that would no doubt lead him back to Genevieve and the kiss they'd once shared. "Well, hopefully you can get things settled down so you can get some rest."

Storm's dark eyes snapped to Zeke's.

"Not that you want things to be *too* settled, of course." Zeke smirked.

"We are quite compatible, if that's what you're implying." The corner of his friend's mouth curled. Zeke could count on one hand the number of times he'd actually seen the man smile. "Very well, in fact." Storm nodded with a far-off look in his eye.

Zeke glanced away. Seeing the lovesick expression on the man he'd sworn would never marry made him…well, uncomfortable. Zeke eyed his friend. "So, you're happy, then?" Zeke asked, praying Storm would spare him the details.

"Oh, sure." He shrugged. "Except for one thing."

Zeke raised his brows and sighed. "What's that?'

"It's her pet goose. At first, he had to sleep at the foot of the bed."

He had to ask. Zeke scratched the back of his neck. As much as Zeke felt for the man on one level, he figured he'd made his own…well, bed and now had to lie in in it--goose and all. Zeke held up his hand. "No need to explain," he offered with an apologetic smile.

"Tell that to my ankles. Godforsaken bird wreaked havoc every time we tried to go to bed. That's why I decided to get him a mate. It worked for a while. He was protective of something else."

Zeke tried to erase the mental image that had formed in his brain.

"Dern thing figured out how to work the handle on the door." Storm glanced away. "You suppose having kids is like that?"

Zeke shrugged, eyeing the door, nervous to move on. "I can't say, my friend." He grasped the man's forearm in a sign of a brotherly solidarity and good will. "Congratulations on your marriage and good luck with the goose…geese," he corrected himself.

Storm chuckled. Both turned as the diner door opened.

"Mr. Kyi-yee," a female voice called from behind him.

Zeke hurried down the street and ducked into the barber's shop, shutting the door firmly behind him. He leaned against it, his heart beating in his throat.

"Good morning," Noelle's one and only barber and occasional dentist, Butch Wisdom greeted him. Broom in hand, he appeared mildly surprised to have such an early customer. "I was just getting ready to open up, if you don't mind waiting a few moments."

Zeke wasn't exactly interested in a shave as much as he was pure survival. Traditionally, women knew better not to enter a barber shop on principle alone. There was a good chance, however, that some silly rule wasn't about to stop Genevieve.

"Good day, Mr. Wisdom. I, uh—just stopped by to see how those pelts I gave you last spring are holding up as rugs?"

The man's brow furrowed. He glanced over Zeke's shoulder. "Excuse me, son. But are you aware there's a fetching-looking woman peering in my shop window. Possible she's looking for you?" Butch took a second look and smiled. "I'm not sure I'd be running away, son."

Zeke debated whether it was time he simply face the music, as it were. Thing was, he didn't know what to say to her. Didn't understand why after all this time just the sight of her put his head into a tailspin. Worse, she wanted him to marry a stranger—a woman he'd never held. Never kissed. Never dreamt for weeks about how sweet was the scent of her skin. Genevieve Walters. What were the odds that the only woman he'd ever truly loved was here in Noelle, Colorado?

"You have a back way out of here?" he asked.

The man glanced at the window and back at Zeke, throwing him a skeptical look. "You sure about that?"

Zeke blew out a sigh. "Not entirely. But it's the best option I've got at the moment."

"Well, unless you got a tooth needing to be tended to." He nodded toward the back. "Through the bathing area. Door leads out back."

"Much appreciated." Zeke strode into the small room containing a fancy porcelain claw-foot tub, a small dresser, and one of his bear pelts spread across the floor. He stood a moment assessing how to get back to his horse and get out of town without running into the good matchmaker. Slowly opening the back door, he peeked out and came face-to-face with the beautiful green-eyed gaze of the woman he'd left out of his own guilt over a dozen years ago.

"Mrs....Walters," he sighed, averting his eyes from her determined gaze.

Chapter Five

Those eyes. If she didn't know better. *But of course, that was impossible.*

"If you'll excuse me, ma'am." The elusive man ducked his head so that her eyes aligned with that of the vacant stare of his bear hood. He scooted quickly around her and headed down the street.

Startled that he'd slipped away so quickly, she blinked, picked up her skirts, and hurried after him. Genevieve stopped on the main street. She searched both ways and found him and his damnable long stride headed around the curve.

He's going to La Maison!

Frustrated, she hiked her skirts once again and hurried across the precariously frozen road to catch up. It would serve him right to discover on his own that Madame and her entourage were no longer at their fancy house, but in the abandoned saloon across the street.

"Mr. Kyo-yee," she shouted against the wind unable to remember the exact pronunciation. It appeared he picked up his pace. With a sigh, Genevieve set her jaw and followed him, catching up to him just before he was about to enter the La Maison. In her haste she grabbed his sleeve.

"Mr. Kyo-yeek." Fiddlesticks, she'd forgotten his name. She hoped he was an understanding man. "Please, may I have but a moment of your time?"

"It is...Kyi-yee." He stood, head bent slightly, staring at La Maison's painted door. Head lowered slightly, his profile resembled a weary bear. "Not Mr. Kyi-yee."

"My apologies, Kyi-yee," she enunciated the name carefully, not wanting to lose his attention again. "Is it a fair assumption, sir, that all of the same things that appeal to most men, appeal also to you?"

His icy blue gaze slid from her hand to her eyes. She dropped her hold and took a step back. Genevieve's thoughts jumbled. She struggled to find them. "Meaning, of course, comforts such as a home-cooked meal, companionship...uh, the matrimonial benefits God designed between a man and a woman."

"You mean *sex*?" He gave her a puzzled frown.

She swallowed. Searched for her brain cells. "Well, yes—in part. Procreation is a fact of life, is it not?" She smiled, though it felt like a million stones sat on her chest.

He glanced at the door. "I think Madame might disagree on the point that sex is only for procreation."

"You are well aware of my meaning, Mr. Kyi-yee. I would appreciate if you would not mock me."

"Your point, Mrs. Walters?"

"Mr. Kyi-yee, *I* can give you those things."

His brows shot up. He tipped his head slightly seeming to study her. She couldn't be certain but she had the feeling that under that thick beard of his was a smirk.

"No, what I meant to say," she bumbled, "is I believe I have just the right woman who could offer you all these things and more, Mr. Kyi-yee. I'm talking, of course, about a lifetime of wedded bliss."

He searched her eyes as though contemplating the offer. It gave Genevieve hope that she'd at least broken through his rugged persona.

"I doubt it." He lifted his hand to the latch, then seemed to change his mind. Turning on his heel he stepped out into the street.

The man, it appeared could be stubborn, but she was as tenacious. She followed and tried to face him but he twisted away, acting as though his attempts to ignore her might wear her down. It only strengthened her resolve. Her passion was her mission, and right now Penelope's happiness was key. "Mr. Kyi-yee, wouldn't you rather know the love of a good woman? A woman you could come home to every night?" She tried to catch his gaze, but he would not have it. He began to walk away. She set her jaw and followed doggedly behind him.

He turned suddenly, causing her to run into his blanket-covered chest. Catching her upper arms, he peered down at her. "Mrs. Walters, I said *no.*"

"What are you doing?" The shrill and none-too-happy voice of Madame Bonheur broke the silence, and tension, between them. She strode across the porch of the crudely built saloon located on the other side of the street from the La Maison des Chats.

Ever since she and the weary-from-travel brides had temporarily taken up residence in the elegantly furnished log building established by madam and her ladies, Genevieve had been advised to stay clear of the disgruntled woman. It was no secret that she was not happy about the transition. She was an intimidating woman—hardened by life, stitched together by survival. Looking every bit like a storm cloud her gaze bore into Genevieve's as she strode toward her, her tight-fitting black dress rustling with each step.

"What is *'appening* here? Do you mean to parlay your situation, *Meezus* Walters? You and your…*scrawny* girls?"

"Parlay my--" Genevieve blinked, realizing her insinuation. "I wouldn't dream of it," she answered. "I was simply discussing an alternative proposition with Mr. Kyi-yee."

Madam frowned. "So, it eez, *Mr.* now, *eez* it?" She nudged his shoulder and offered him a savvy wink.

The man simply shook his head and looked away.

"If you are quite finished, I'd like to take my client inside. He looks in need of a *beet* of…refreshing, shall we say?" Madam slipped her arm through his.

"And I was just offering that he could have such refreshment on a nightly basis with what I have to offer." Genevieve crossed her arms in an effort to make her point.

Madame's ruby red lips curled into a smile. "*Weeth* such ambition, my dear, perhaps you should come work for Madame?"

Genevieve frowned. "Oh, not me, Madame. One of my brides."

Madame snorted. "I have heard that one of your grooms left town. You won't be taking *theez* one from us, *mon cherry*. He *eez* madame's Monsieur Charmant." She puckered her lips and made a smooching sound.

Mr. Charming? Genevieve, who'd had schooling in French, found Madame's mastery of the language lacking, but she refused to humiliate the woman. She had greater concerns. For instance, she needed Madame to release the man she needed as a prospective groom.

"Excuse me, Madam. Mrs. Walters." Kyi-yee pulled away from the woman's grasp. He sighed and glanced from one woman to the other. "Ladies, I wish I could say this has been a pleasure." He eyed them. "If you'll excuse me."

"Oh, now, Ze--" Madam started.

His finger darted to her lips, silencing her. "Another time, Madame." He tipped his head, glanced at Genevieve, and strode again towards town.

Madame tossed Genevieve a stern glare, flipped her shawl around her shoulders. "You would do well, *Meesuz* Walters not to interfere with the men who were wise enough not to volunteer for *theez* ridiculous *leetle* game the pastor created. It will not work, you know." Her stern gaze flicked over Genevieve before she turned with a huff and walked back to her temporary palace of sin. She glanced up at the array of women along the balcony railing who'd sauntered out to watch the encounter, dressed scantily in their undergarments. "I do not pay you to stand outside," she called, waving at them. "Back inside, now. I don't need you all to catch a chill. The sneezing is bad for *beeznus*."

Maybe it was useless. Maybe she didn't have a prayer. What was it that Pastor Hammond had told her? *When one door closes, God opens another?* Well, perhaps Mr. Kyi-yee—the stubborn old-so-and-so—didn't realize yet that *he'd* been the one to walk through that door. Surely, he couldn't argue with divine intervention?

She glanced at his departing form. What now? Perhaps Madame had been right, despite her poor French and penchant for lust. Maybe she was wrong to bring women here who might not be as well-equipped as she thought to deal with this new frontier.

Then again, it was the season of miracles. She needed to find Pastor Hammond and convince him she'd laid for him a proper foundation. It was now his job to explain to Mr. Kyi-yee what fulfilling this agreement would mean for the town and its residents.

Breathless from her urgent walk, Genevieve pushed open the door of the Golden Nugget. She blinked, her eyes adjusting to the dim shadows. Kerosene lamps flickered on the tables. The scent of the wood-burning stove, male sweat, and whiskey hung in the closed quarters of the saloon.

She wove through the tables, reset from earlier in the day, filled now with patrons playing cards, drinking and, in general, taking advantage of the slow down at the mine.

Seamus Malone leaned on his bar as she approached. "Aye, Mrs. Walters. Did *ya* manage *ta* wrangle a groom for Miss Penny?"

Genevieve glanced over her shoulder catching the curious gaze of a table of men playing cards. They quickly refocused on their game.

Genevieve sighed. "I'm going to need Pastor Hammond's aid in convincing Mr. Kyi-yee," she said. "Unless, by some chance, *you* might be looking for a wife, *dear* Mr. Malone?" She eyed the handsome bartender.

Seamus lowered his gaze, pretending to be polishing his beloved bar. "Might I ask ye for a bit of advice, ma'am? You being a matchmaker, and all."

"For a cup of coffee, Mr. Malone. I would gladly welcome the reprieve."

He nodded toward a small table near the Christmas tree. "I'll get us some coffee. Ye go have a seat there where we can chat in private."

She gazed at the festive tree and thought of her recent encounter with the mountain man they called Kyi-yee. A man who, from all appearances, seemed comfortable conversing with others but could not seem to carry on a conversation of two minutes with her. In fact, he could barely look at her in the eye.

Chapter Six

The fierce thudding of Zeke's heart pounded against his chest, reminiscent of the sound of the rock crusher, called the Drum--at the mine. He felt like a coward. Able to face a ferocious bear, but not the woman he'd once sworn his heart to. Just the same he was relieved to have slipped away from the clutches of the two quarreling women before Madame foolishly blurted out his real name.

Seeing her, being so close and yet afraid to admit he still cared for her was an unbearable torture to his soul. Crushing. Smashing. Until he thought he might not be able to breathe. He'd made up his mind never to marry again. Once…seeing the horror on his new bride's face—was enough of a jolt to his pride. Besides, so much time had gone by. They'd both changed. He was acutely aware of the scars he bore both inside and out. Genevieve had moved on. What right did he have to resurface now, or perhaps risk her rejection? Besides, a woman of Genevieve's upbringing, her stature, deserved more than a scarred body and a man who lived like a hermit in the hills.

Feelings he'd so carefully folded away over time caused his chest to ache, and his to body burn with a desire that not even a visit to La Maison would quench. Memories plagued his mind—the taste of her lips, the soft sound in her throat as he held her close. Zeke pressed his eyes shut, willing the past to remain where it belonged. Things were different now. He had to accept that.

He glanced up from where he'd ducked into the shadows of a building waiting and watching until he'd seen Genevieve walk past. The look of defeat on her face, the resignation--it appeared she'd finally given up. That was as it should be.

Then why did it hurt so damn much?

He spotted Pastor Hammond going into the barber shop. Curious, to find out what all this marriage ruckus meant for Noelle and for the woman who seemed to be at the center of the chaos, he followed the preacher inside.

Butch glanced up in surprise. "Change your mind about that shave? I can get to you right after I finish here with the preacher," he said snapping open a cloth and laying it over the pastor's torso.

Pastor Hammond glanced at Zeke and offered a friendly smile.

"We need to talk, preacher," Zeke said, pulling up a chair.

"That's all well and good, if you don't mind me going ahead with my shave," Pastor Hammond said.

Butch waited, cup and brush poised.

Zeke nodded.

Butch began to lather the preacher's face.

"I want to know what's going on in this town." Zeke peered at the man whose lower face had transformed to a soapy white.

"I presume you are referring to the matchmaker woman and the good number of our businessmen in town who are recently married?"

"To start with," Zeke said. He leaned his chair against the wall and waited for the preacher's explanation.

"You may or may not be aware that there has been little evidence of gold in the mine in some time now. Concern is that it's dried up."

Zeke raised a brow. "That's interesting. You can usually hear the drum for miles through these mountains. Has he closed the mine?"

Pastor shook his head. "Oh no. On the contrary, Charles Hardt is most determined to prove otherwise. A good number of miners have already left town, searching for new strikes elsewhere. try to stake their claim elsewhere. The drum's shut down and the crew left were let off today to attend the foreman's wedding."

Zeke nodded. "I happen to run into Silas Powell early this morning. Said something about hearing of another strike. He seemed in a hurry. That would explain it. Can't say that riding alone is a very wise thing to do these days."

Pastor Hammond sighed. "Dern fool is liable to get himself killed."

"Or worse," Zeke added raising a brow.

Silence filled the room as the trio absorbed Zeke's words.

"Well, for the folks that have chosen to stay, who've created their businesses here, this town means more than a gold strike. Sure, it's why they settled here, most, anyhow--to take advantage of the claim. But they chose to settle down and make a life in this little spot where they've worked and lived for the past couple of years."

Zeke thought of what it'd been like when he and Clem had arrived. Back then, Noelle was no more than a handful of tents and ramshackle buildings. With each new wagon train filled with men coming to work in the mine, they brought not only dreams of striking it rich, but their individual ingenuity and determination as well. It didn't take long for Charles Hardt, owner of the mine, to tap into the human resources he had and begin to slowly build a town. There was much that could still be achieved to make it habitable, but the progress over the past couple of years was evident.

"Do you believe the mine is dried up?" Zeke asked.

Pastor Hammond seemed to debate the thought. "Well, whether or not they find more gold in the mine, there are now those who consider Noelle their home. And if, say, the railroad was to bring their line through Noelle and take it further west, it would be a boon for all involved."

Zeke listened, beginning to realize what the reverend had been trying to accomplish.

Pastor Hammond caught Zeke's gaze, pulling him from his previous thoughts. "I'd heard you lost your brother here in Noelle."

Zeke looked away, the memories still fresh in his mind. His brother's laugh, how ornery he could be. How much he loved being out here--being his own boss, a real pioneer. Clem's death wasn't a topic he discussed with anyone. And he'd never spoken to a man of the cloth about it. "Yessir. It was…an accident."

"My sincere condolences, son. It's never easy to lose someone or something you love."

"It was the mine," Zeke blurted out, surprised by the bitter taste on his tongue.

The pastor waved away Butch when he offered a spicy aftershave. He turned his attention to Zeke. "And a man in your position would have every reason not to care whether the mine, this town, or its people stay or blow away in a cloud of dust." He nodded and breathed a quiet sigh. "Perfectly understandable."

Zeke stared at his boots. The memory of his brother's enthusiastic expression when he came home from the mine haunted him still. He'd never seen a man more alive as Clem was when he went to work every day at the mine. In the evenings, Zeke would find him seated on the front porch of the cabin they'd built with their own hands. He'd be holding a cup of coffee and staring at the sunset. "He loved it here," Zeke said. "The river, the trees, the mountains…that damn mine. It was like some grand adventure to him" Zeke glanced at the preacher, his heart twisted with guilt. Why hadn't he insisted that a more seasoned man volunteer that day? He'd been the foreman. Clem had been adamant about setting the charges…. "He'd never have lasted had he stayed on the farm. Always had his damn head in the clouds. Wanting to travel, see new places." The memory of that day served like a knife, plunging deep into Zeke's heart.

***

"Come on, Zeke. Look, not another man has offered to set the charges." Clem's enthusiasm for this mine was beyond anything Zeke understood. Up at the crack of dawn, pickax and lantern in hand, heading into that black hole of a mountain.

"You heard the boss. If we want to save time before the cold weather hits, we need to use charges to get farther inside the mountain. I'm good at this, Zeke--you know I am. I can get in there and out faster and more efficiently than any man here," Clem pleaded with his brother.

Zeke scratched the back of his neck and scanned the other members of his scraggly crew. He looked at Clem. "I'll do it." Zeke started walking toward the wagon loaded with dynamite. They needed to only set a few to create some exploratory holes.

"I'll flip you for it. Heads I win, tails you lose."

Zeke looked over his shoulder. "What kind of a fool do you take me for?"

Clem shrugged his shoulders and gave him a wicked grin. The crew was waiting. Clem was five years younger than Zeke and thankfully hadn't enlisted when the war broke out at the insistence of their father who needed him on the farm.

Zeke turned on his heel and winced. An old injury to his knee caused him fits now and again if he turned it the wrong way. Clenching his back teeth, he limped back to Clem. His brother raised his chin, holding his gaze steady.

"You're not going to be able to get out of there fast enough with that bum knee of yours." Clem nodded toward Zeke's leg.

"I think we should send a more seasoned man," Zeke countered. He scanned the crew. Not a soul piped up to volunteer; most looked down at the ground.

Clem glanced around and then looked back at Zeke. "There's your answer, sir. How many charges do I need to set?"

Zeke hated conceding to his younger brother, but he had little choice. "Three. That's it. We just need to blow some exploratory holes, nothing more. You make sure they have long fuses, light them, and get your ass back out here. Don't look back, don't hesitate. Do you understand?"

Zeke limped beside him, barking out instructions as Clem gathered the dynamite in his bag and slung it over his shoulder.

He faced Zeke and clamped a hand down over his shoulder. "No different than lighting firecrackers down at the founder's fair back home." Clem smiled. "You remember how we made Peggy Overton scream when we blew her picnic basket to bits?"

"I remember not being able to sit for a week after Pa finished with us," Zeke answered with a grin. He sobered quickly. "Clem, this isn't firecrackers."

"Ah, go on. You sound like Ma. I'll get this set and be out in time to beat you—again—at a game of checkers tonight." He patted Zeke's shoulder as he walked around him and entered the dark hole in the side of the mountain.

An icy dread filled Zeke's stomach. He'd instructed the crew to wait a few yards back from the opening behind some larger boulders. His mind was quickly calculating the firepower of the three sticks of dynamite. Clem could do it. It seemed as though Zeke's heart halted, as did his breathing. His gaze was fixed on the yawning black mouth of the mine, willing his brother to emerge. One minute, then two…no explosion. No Clem. Maybe they were faulty. Zeke wiped his brow and sighed. He should be out here by now. Three minutes had passed. Four. Zeke scanned the score of men crouched down, waiting. "Where's Storm Thornton?"

"Dern half-breed probably still in there." He heard one of the miners say under his breath.

Zeke stood, preparing to give the man a lesson in consideration.

"Be prepared to buy me drinks at the Nugget," Zeke heard Clem's disembodied voice echoing through the dark shadows of the tunnel.

Zeke released a relieved breath and smiled. "Smart ass," he hollered. "You and Storm get your asses out here."

Then the world shattered. A plume of thick black smoke rolled from the entrance. Bits of rock, sharp as arrows, pelted the crew. They all ducked, shielding themselves behind the boulder.

Zeke was already running toward the mine, fighting through the residual haze and debris. Dust coated his throat as he called out to his brother. Pain shot up his leg, his eyes burned. Blindly, he stumbled toward where the opening should be. It was filled in with rubble. "Clem!" he yelled, tossing aside the broken landslide of jagged rock. "Clem!" One by one the crew joined in helping move the layers of crushed rock. Zeke's fingers bled, his back burned, but he would find him, by God. "You there," he barked at one of the crew. "Run and get Doc Deane." He scanned the shocked faces of his crew. "Keep digging."

What seemed like hours later, they'd removed tons of rock, and still there was no sign of his brother or Storm Thornton. Faces caked with dirt and sweat looked to Zeke for guidance. Hope of finding either man alive had begun to dwindle.

"Keep digging. No one leaves this mine until both men are found. Do you understand?" It was not a request. Pain, fear drove Zeke on. Years of fighting a senseless war, of watching brother fight brother, family against family had left him grateful that Clem had been spared the horror.

Now this.

Zeke fought back the tears, the frustration and guilt. There was no time. Each moment was precious. Each stone tossed aside gave renewed hope that Clem would be found alive.

"I see him," one man called from the other side of the pile of rock that had been cast aside.

Zeke steeled himself, rounding the rocks piled higher than him. He closed his eyes, saying a prayer that by some miracle his brother had survived.

But there would be no miracles that day.

They dragged his broken body from beneath the rubble. Zeke stared down at what had once been a thriving, full-of-life man. Some turned away. Others lost the contents of their stomachs. Zeke could only stare and blame himself. "It should have been me. You bastard, why did it have to be you?" He dropped to his knees and picked up his brother's body in his arms. Great sobs racked his body as he rocked his baby brother. He raised his eyes to the heavens, to the pristine blue sky and the brilliant sun that his brother so dearly loved. "Dammit. Why did you have to take him and not me?" he cursed the heavens.

The rest was a watery blur. He remembered barking at the stunned men to keep digging, to find Storm even as Doc Deane and Charles Hardt tried to pry Clem from his arms. He barely remembered the wagon ride back to town and he remembered sending up a fleeting prayer that Storm would be found. Laying his brother's lifeless body on the doctors table, he collapsed and his world went black until he woke the next day in a bed at Doc's office.

Against the advice of the good doctor, he'd retrieved Clem's body and discovered that Jack Peregrine had fashioned for him a practical and sturdy coffin. There were those who wanted a ceremony—wanted to pay their respects. Zeke refused. Anger and guilt shoved the rest of the world away. He wanted no help, no comfort, least of all from God at that time. No. He buried Clem alone and spent the better part of the day staring at the marker he'd made of stones and hating Clem for being such a stubborn, cocky ass of a brother. He sobbed until his body was sore, punishing himself until he had no more left in him for tears. Only guilt remained.

He started walking at some point—up the mountainside. He had no idea what he was looking for, what he was running from. But something inside drove him forward as though searching for the demon that had sucked the life from him. He found it deep in the woods late that day as the sun cast dusky shadows in the deep forest atop a ridge. A slobbering eight-foot demon with snapping teeth and claws that made ribbons of his flesh. The last thing Zeke remembered was feeling the hot breath of the grizzly against his cheek and thinking he was about to die.

Chapter Seven

Those eyes.

Another man's eyes pulled at Genevieve's memory. A moment in time that she'd tucked away never thinking it might be resurrected—the stranger who had shown up on her doorstep bringing her news from the war. A promise he'd made to her husband—his commanding officer—to return the letters she'd written, along with his watch, should anything happen to him.

This blue-eyed soldier spoke of her husband in such high esteem that she'd wondered what he'd understood about Levi Walters that she hadn't. The soldier spoke of her letters, about how he'd read them to her husband each night as his captain lay weary from battle.

She was humbled, and quite possibly guilty of being more enamored by the young soldier's praise of her loyalty, resiliency, and devotion to her husband. He confessed how the letters that he'd been privy to had helped him, as well, through many a difficult time at war. Lonely and perhaps needing solace, she had been stirred by his kind words, his admiration. There had been an undeniable attraction between them.

When in a single desperate moment, they'd kissed--forbidden and too soon after her husband's death—she'd felt evidence of his desire in his passionate embrace. He had aroused emotions inside her that she'd never felt for her husband. Had it been another time, another place, they might have shared more intimately what the kiss had begun. Yet with that stolen kiss, Genevieve knew no other man would ever hold her heart like Sergeant Christian Ezekiel Kinnison. Deep down, she knew it was wrong to have such feelings and somehow, she knew he would not wish to put her—nor himself —through such misery. By morning, he'd gone. Headed west as he'd told her, to follow his brother. She'd never shared what had happened between them with another soul, nor the way her heart had broken when he went away.

When she'd awoken the next day to find the young soldier gone, Genevieve had realized that her marriage had been a shell, nothing more than an arrangement between her parents and his. With the war looming, they'd met only once before the wedding. Within the week he'd been called to war.

Early on, he'd been able to return on furlough a handful of occasions when time and proximity allowed. His conversations were most always of battle. Rarely, if ever, did he mention how he'd missed her, or what her letters had meant to him. And though he performed his husbandly duty, by dawn he was off again to his precious war.

The scent of strong coffee brought her back to the present.

"Tis a shame Silas did what he did, Mrs. Walters. Some men aren't the marrying kind, I 'spect." Seamus, the Nugget's bartender, sat two steaming mugs on the table and waited until Genevieve had sat down before seating himself. She found the simple gesture endearing, so unlike his usual cantankerous behavior.

"And you, Mr. Malone? Are you not the marrying kind?" Genevieve asked. She held the cup in both hands, grateful for its warmth. Glad for a few moments to gather her strategy in finding Penny a husband.

His gaze remained on his cup. "The thing is ma'am, I am married—or I was."

Genevieve frowned, her heart going out to the man. "I'm sorry, Mr. Malone. What happened?"

He glanced up then, averting his gaze as though unable to face her. "Oh, she's alive and well. Last I knew she was still living back East."

Genevieve studied the silver just beginning to appear at the man's temples. He couldn't be more than his mid-thirties, but life out here had a way of aging a man beyond his years.

His gaze flickered back to hers. She saw his embarrassment.

"I've been sending her money, but to tell you the truth watching all these men getting married has made me miss her something fierce. I'd like to send for her." He turned the cup in his hands and took a quick sip. "If she'll have me again, that is."

Curiosity laced with compassion caused Genevieve to reach out and cover Seamus's hand wrapped around his cup. "How can I help, Mr. Malone?"

He seemed to struggle with opening up to her. He laid his hands firmly on the table, his eyes meeting hers. "The truth is Mrs. Walters, she gave me the boot."

"The boot? What would possess her to do such a thing, Mr. Malone?"

"Aye, because I was a drinkin' bastard, ma'am," he lamented, then seemed to remember his manners. "My apologies, ma'am."

"Accepted, Mr. Malone. Do you feel up to sharing what happened?"

He dismissed her concern with a wave of his hand. "To be sure, the woman had every right to do as she did. I was up to no good back then, ma'am. Worthless, I was…and that's bein' kind about it."

Her heart went out to his confession. It must have taken great courage to face his demons and admit to them. Certainly, he was not the grumbling curmudgeon he often portrayed himself to be. "What changed for you, Mr. Malone?" She studied him. "You don't at all seem to be the man you've described."

He nodded. "My humble thanks, ma'am." He stared over her shoulder as though formulating his thoughts. "But if I were to name one thing, I would say it was this town. Noelle, ma'am." He chuckled softly. "Now you take Mr. Hardt, for example--there is a fine man, a gracious man. Not everyone thinks as much, and he is tough—there's no question to that." The regard for his boss was evident in his eyes. He tapped his finger to the table. "I made it out this far and had no idea where to go. He offered me a job, helping him run the bar." He took a sip of his coffee. "When the mine began to take up more of his time, he handed over the reins to me. *Me.*" He smiled. "Who'd have believed such a thing? I knew it was my chance to get my life right and since the day he hired me, I've not had a drink." His thoughtful gaze narrowed. "I suppose you could say Noelle saved me, Mrs. Walters."

His confession touched her in a way unexpected. Perhaps there was more to this little town than what the eye could see. She realized that, in part, Pastor Hammond's description, while far different than what reality offered, came from perhaps a similar perspective. Maybe it was why he wrote of such an idyllic place. She sniffed, surprised by the emotions it jarred inside her. Genevieve smiled. "You're as fine a man as I've had the pleasure to meet, Seamus Malone."

The flesh above his beard blushed crimson.

"How may I help you?" she asked, determined now to do her best to bring happiness to him.

He slipped a piece of paper from his pocket, unfolded it, and handed it to her. On it was an address, faded with time. "I was hopin' that you might consider writing to my wife. You know, put in a good word as a matchmaker, about how I am now. Help me tell her how I feel. Ask her to come to Noelle and give me another chance?"

Genevieve studied the sincerity on the man's face. "I will do what I can to help you, Mr. Malone. But I must get through the next two days. You do understand, don't you?"

He tapped his fingers to the table again and nodded. "I do. Most obliged, ma'am. Well, I best be getting' back ta work, then."

She watched him walk away and took a sip of the stout coffee he'd brought her.

"Mrs. Walters? Ma'am, may I have a moment of your time?"

Puzzled, she peered over the mug at the stranger standing before her. A tall, lanky fellow with a thick, dark moustache. His hat was tattered at the edges. The simple undershirt he wore was pock-marked with stains. It was, however, the utter and open look of earnestness in the man's dark brown eyes that captured her attention. "The name's Orvis Weston, ma'am." He removed his hat to reveal dark hair, silvery at the temples, cut neatly at the neck and above the ears.

"Please, have a seat, Mr. Weston." She nodded to the empty chair across from her. She wasn't certain how appropriate it was to meet with not one, but two men in a saloon. Still, she was in a public place, and on Sunday's and special occasions it was considered church. Besides, it was becoming clear that this little town might benefit from her expertise.

"Ma'am, I've been watching the weddings all week." He held his hat, turning it nervously between his hands. "I wasn't chosen to be a groom, ma'am."

Genevieve's interest piqued. "Do you have an interest in getting married, Mr. Weston?" This might well solve her issue with Penelope. Perhaps she'll have two men to choose from?

"Yes, ma'am." He swallowed. "I surely am."

"And you'd like my help in finding you a bride?" She smiled. "Well, Mr. Weston, as it happens, I may be able to help you."

He cleared his throat and his gaze darted to the table of men playing cards across the room. "Appreciate that, ma'am. But thing is…I already found me the woman I want to marry. I just don't quite know how to go about it."

Perplexed, Genevieve eyed the man. From the table nearby came the muffled sound of laughter.

"Y'all can just hush." His drawl, decidedly southern, warned his card-playing friends. He glanced at Genevieve. "Pay them no mind, ma'am. They don't know what it feels like."

"Feels like, Mr. Weston?" she asked, suddenly wishing she had a drink of Seamus's amber-colored courage from behind the bar.

"Bein' in love, ma'am," he said searching her eyes.

"I see." Genevieve placed her hands in her lap. "Why don't you tell me a little bit about this woman? Have you corresponded at some length with her?"

More muffled laughter.

Orvis leaned forward and spoke in a hushed voice. "We've been corresponding a great deal, ma'am. She's right here in Noelle."

She raised her brows and searched her mind to what other women she'd seen in town. There were very few other than the woman she'd brought from Denver. There was, of course, Madame and her ladies at La Maison. "Is it one of the women I brought with me, Mr. Weston?" There was only two women left—Penelope and Agatha. And Agatha had been spending far too much time with Madame since the man chosen as her groom--eighty-year-old farmer had taken one look at her and vehemently decided that at seventy-five years old, she was too young for him. The crotchety old man spat a wad of chew on the ground, turned on his boot heel and went back to his ranch in the hills where he raised goats. Agatha was beyond relieved stating, "I don't want a man who expects me to cook and clean. The men who frequent La Maison are just interested in getting down to business." She'd declared her independence to Genevieve two days after their arrival, leaving her short of the twelve needed to satisfy the contract. That was before Silas deserted the cause in search of gold.

Now two spots remained and only two days to fill them.

Weston lowered his voice and scooted his chair closer. "No, ma'am."

Genevieve held her breath, managing a weak smile.

"It's Miss Boum Boum."

Genevieve straightened, unsure if she'd heard the man correctly. She paused to find a delicate way to ask. "Do you mean the woman who claims she can balance two tea cups on her--" She gestured loosely toward the man's chest.

A grin split his face. "Yes, ma'am. She's the one."

Unexpected as this was, the real challenge now faced her. Did she help this man gain Miss Boum Boum's hand in marriage—no easy task given that Madame—while portraying the considerate boss, behaved more like a warden to her ladies.

Or...

Try her best in talking him into marrying Penny.

She caught the man's longing gaze. Penny would never do. No woman except the soiled dove at La Maison would satisfy this love-struck southerner. That left her with no choice but a probable confrontation with Madame Bonheur.

On the other hand, were it to be a successful union in which she played her part, it's possible the railroad might consider the marriage to be in compliance with the original agreement. "How well do you know this woman, Mr. Weston?" Genevieve's desire to affirm both parties were like-minded was a natural concern.

Orvis's smile was shy. He blushed a little as he grinned. "I 'spect I know her about as well as a man can know a woman, ma'am."

It was Genevieve's turn to blush. She cleared her throat. "What I mean is does Miss Boum Boum feel similarly?"

He blinked, tossing her a frown.

"Does she feel as you do, Mr. Weston?"

"Oh." He nodded. "Yes, ma'am. She sure does. I knew there was something different about her the first time I laid eyes on her. Did you know she has many talents, Mrs. Walters? I could give you a list of the things she has shown me. You'd be mighty impressed, as I was." In his excitement, his voice rose.

So, too, the laughter from the men playing cards.

Genevieve cringed at seeing the man's humiliation. Seeking to restore his dignity she spoke with clear intention. "Mr. Weston, it is my belief that everyone deserves to be happy. And if you and Miss Boum Boum have found such happiness together then I will do all in my power to help the both of you."

His smile showed genuine relief. He clasped his hands and blinked a couple of times, fighting back his emotions. With a nod, he pushed to his feet. "I'll tell her what you said." He held his hat, appearing uncertain whether to shake her hand or hug her. "I'm mighty obliged to you, Mrs. Walters. Mighty obliged."

Chapter Eight

Zeke's eyes rose to meet the pastor's concerned gaze.

"I don't know where your mind took you just now, son. I suspect nowhere good. Thing you need to know is that your brother's death wasn't your fault. It was an accident. Nothing more." The preacher offered a quiet smile. "That cemetery out there is full of men who had the same dream as your brother. I suppose when you think about it, they made the ultimate sacrifice in trying to find their place in this world. The folks here in Noelle, they're no different. But it's those men to whom we owe a great debt. It's our job to carry on and create that dream they sought and do so in their memory. Wouldn't you agree?"

Zeke understood clearly now what was the purpose of their plan. He sighed, his soul feeling purged of the guilt he'd been carrying around. It hurt still—it hurt like hell. But he no longer felt alone. He only had to ask himself if he loved Noelle as much as his brother had. Did he have the courage to carry on his brother's dream and help create the town Clem would have been proud to call home? Zeke glanced at Pastor Hammond. This was Clem's home now—it would be forever. Zeke owed him that much. But there was still the matter of Genevieve Walters. She had no idea of his identity. She too had moved on—perhaps even had someone back in Denver waiting for her. "What about the matchmaker?" Zeke asked.

Pastor Hammond tossed him a perplexed look.

"What does she stand to gain from all of this?"

"Ah," the pastor said with a nod. He stood and slipped his hat off the crude hat rack nailed to the wall. "As I am to understand, there were not many who believed Mrs. Walters had the capability to follow through with these marriages. Or, rather, see them to a successful completion. I imagine that marrying off these women would be a feather in her cap back at the Benevolent Society of Lost Souls." He chuckled. "I haven't seen the men in this town so productive and enthusiastic since I've been here. We're hoping of course, their enthusiasm will spread to the other single men in town and if all goes well, we hope to employ Mrs. Walters help again." He shook his head. "I've never seen a woman with such dedication to her work." He looked at Zeke. "She's a widow, you know. Never married again. Devoted her life to helping others find happiness. She told me she still carries her husband's letters from the war. They were given to her by a young soldier--

apparently one of her husband's officers who'd brought them to her along with the news of his passing." Pastor Hammond tapped his hat on his head, then fished out a coin and tossed it to Butch. "I've had to write many a letter informing family of the death of a loved one, and that in itself is a difficult task." He studied the ground. "I've never had to tell a woman to her face that she's just become a widow. And after all that young man had probably seen on top of that."

The preacher looked, then at Zeke, the kindness in his gaze slicing through the wall Zeke had built around his heart.

"That had to have taken a great deal of courage under fire," the pastor said.

Zeke looked away.

Pastor Hammond cleared his throat. "Well, at any rate, I suspect that when Mrs. Walters returns to Denver with news of her success the tithes at Eastertide will be a little fatter. That will please her superiors in the clergy."

Zeke's chest weighed heavy realizing the extent to which Genevieve had poured herself into her mission. The thought that came next was for her. Maybe out of guilt, but also out of a true desire to help her mission be a success. "How much time is left?"

Pastor Hammond gave Zeke a surprised look. He pulled out an old pocket watch and gazed a few seconds at it. "According to Percival who is constantly reminding me, I'd say we're down to a couple of days. We'd had a wedding scheduled for earlier today" --Pastor Hammond shrugged—"but that didn't exactly go as planned. Not entirely sure how we're going to meet our deadline. All the wedding certificates must be signed and witnessed before the morning of January 6th" He glanced at Zeke and offered a hopeful smile. "I'd like to think God provides."

"And if all the criteria are not fulfilled by that time, what then?" Zeke asked.

Pastor Hammond drew his hand over his mouth and sighed. "Well, no rail line will come through Noelle. What business there is will slow down to a crawl. Most folks will try to hold on for as long as possible. But eventually, like so many towns started by mining, they'll be forced to move on." He glanced at Zeke. "In short, Noelle will die a slow and painful death."

Zeke couldn't take back the past or the years since. Genevieve had gone on with her life—found a passion that she believed in with helping others. And despite that, he was aggravated that at every turn most of the friends he'd made it seemed had married. And were he to be truthful with himself, he was envious, too--envious that they'd had the courage to follow through, to take a risk in order to save something they loved. Noelle. Maybe he, too, was worthy of love. With guilt gnawing at his gut, but with a greater desire to help Genevieve's cause, he met the preacher's gaze. "In your opinion, preacher, is Penelope Jackson an understanding woman?"

The Pastor shrugged, pondering the question. He smiled. "Mrs. Walters has a high regard for her—that says a lot, right there. She seems like a very patient and kind person. Mrs. Walters says with the right man she would--"

"I'll marry Penelope Jackson."

Pastor Hammond's eyes narrowed as he tipped his head. "Pardon, but did I hear you say that you'd marry Miss Penelope?"

Zeke nodded. He pushed away that it was a ridiculous idea, in favor of the noble perspective of helping Genevieve succeed. "I will need to get cleaned up first."

"Fine idea. Shave and a bath. Two bits." Butch grinned.

Zeke shook his head. "Need to finish up a few things first." He looked at the preacher. "Where and when, Pastor Hammond?"

Pastor Hammond looked perplexed, but offered a grin. "The Golden Nugget, let's say eleven-thirty tonight? That will give me time to speak with Seamus about closing up early."

Zeke nodded, opened the door and peered out. He looked over his shoulder at the dumbfounded expression on Pastor Hammond's face. "I have one final request about this."

The pastor nodded. "Of course, what is it?"

"I ask only that the matchmaker not be present at the ceremony." Zeke waited, gauging the man's reaction. He saw the uncertainty in the preacher's expression. "Or we don't have a deal, agreed?"

The struggle was plain on Pastor Hammond's face. "I'll do my best, son."

Chapter Nine

Elated by the sudden turn of events, Genevieve eyed the Christmas tree in the saloon and pondered if Providence had once more intervened.

In his exuberance, Orvis had swung open the saloon door and nearly bowled over Pastor Hammond. They danced around each other until finally the preacher stepped aside and with a tip of his hat allowed the excited man to pass.

The wind had calmed by late morning, though the sky had remained mottled gray with patches of blue. The maudlin skies didn't dampen Genevieve's mood, however. She had much to share with the preacher. "Pastor Hammond," Genevieve said as she stood to greet him. "I have some delightful news."

Hat in hand, the preachers countenance showed equal excitement. "What a difference a few hours can make, Mrs. Walters. I also have news that I feel is most joyous." He stood at the table smiling, but wholly out of breath. "May we sit? I dang near ran back up the street hoping to find you." He rounded the table and held her chair for her. "Pray tell, Mrs. Walters. You look about to burst. Has there been word of Silas? Has he returned?"

Genevieve frowned. "No, I'm afraid we've seen the last of Silas in Noelle and I doubt Penelope would reconsider even if he were to return." She smiled. "No, Pastor Hammond, what is done is done. However, there may be another way to resolve our problem." She paused and took a deep breath. "I've just been speaking to Mr. Weston, the man you ran into at the door."

The Pastor grinned. "And he has agreed to marry Penelope?"

"Not exactly." Genevieve shrugged. "It would seem that Mr. Weston is quite taken with one of Madame Bonheur's ladies." She watched his expression to gauge his reaction. He had, after all, been the one to warn against becoming involved with the madam at all costs. "A vindictive woman," he'd said. "Not the kind you want to tangle with."

Pastor turned his hand up to stop her. "Mrs. Walters, we spoke about Madame and agreed not to cause any more of a stir than has already occurred."

Genevieve feared that many concessions had to have been made to appease Madame's moving her business into the old, abandoned saloon across the street from La Maison—no matter how temporary their residency.

Genevieve met his concerned gaze. "Nonetheless, Pastor Hammond, this may well be the miracle we've been looking for."

He gave her the signature grin that could charm the corset off a saloon girl—were he not a man of the cloth.

"You mentioned that you had some news?" she asked.

He sat forward. "Indeed, I do. I was just at the barber and Kyi-yee walked in. We spoke for some time. Did you know that his brother was killed here at the mine shortly after they arrived? Tragic." He shook his head. "He wouldn't say much about it, but I could see from the look in his eyes that the memories are still fresh."

Genevieve raised her brows. Of course, she had no knowledge of the man other than he smelled like a three-day carcass and bore more fur than a wooly mammoth. That, and the fact, that he'd avoided her attempts to speak with him as though she had the plague. "I had no idea," she said, then considered the trauma in the man's life. "Do you find him fit…mentally, emotionally, Pastor Hammond?" Imposing unexpected issues on any of her ladies wouldn't be fair, even though Kyi-yee had several times declined her proposal.

He paused with a reflective stance. "I think he has met his demons for the most part. He asked a great many questions about the contract with the rail line. We discussed what it would mean for Noelle. Oddly enough, he asked about you."

"Me?" That did surprise her. Although, giving it a second thought, it might not seem so strange given that she'd chased him like a fool all over town. Still, her curiosity was piqued. Conversing with the hairy man couldn't be the miracle the preacher referred to, although it was possible. "And, more to the point, what is this miracle, Pastor Hammond?" She nudged him from his reverie.

"Oh, yes. Yes." He dismissed his pondering with a wave of his hand. "It seems that Mr. Kyi-yee is willing to marry Penelope Jackson. Whatever you said to him must have persuaded his change of heart. Well done, Mrs. Walters." He patted her hand.

No one was more surprised than her. "That is most odd, Pastor Hammond. Since I spent more time chasing after him rather than talking. In fact, it seemed his goal was to escape me at every turn."

The preacher's joyful expression turned confused. He appeared deep in thought. "It's strange. He did make an odd request, come to think of it."

"Of course, one might expect some concessions—compromises, if you will—under the circumstances. What is it?" she asked.

Pastor Hammond eyed her with a tip of his head. "He asked that you not be present at the ceremony."

He might just as well as dumped a bucket of icy water over her head. "What on earth? Why?" she sputtered. "It's imperative I be there. She's one of my ladies. I have to be there."

Pastor Hammond raised a brow. "Well, now," he said, speaking slow and easy, "technically, we could get another witness. And legally-speaking, only my name is required on the certificate."

Genevieve sat in stunned silence. "I...I don't know what to say—how I should respond. I--this is utterly ridiculous."

Pastor Hammond lifted his hands and shrugged. "Compromise, Mrs. Walters. Think here of the greater good to come of this."

"Those were his terms?" she asked.

He hesitated, studying her. "Yes ma'am. And I agreed to them, because I thought you'd agree to them as well. After all, the point here is getting Penelope married, isn't that true?"

Genevieve stood and paced the floor as she thought.

"Mrs. Walters? Is this going to be an issue?" Pastor Hammond had a worried look in his eye.

"Where is that insufferable man, now?" she asked, prepared to hunt him down and give him a piece of her mind.

"He's gone home to get ready for the wedding. He's coming here to the saloon by eleven-thirty." He glanced around her. "Which reminds me, I need to speak with Seamus and ask him to clear the place later this evening for a service." He stood and tucked his hands in his vest pockets. "Do I have your word, Mrs. Walters that you'll do nothing to disrupt tonight's plans? The fate of Noelle may well rest on it."

Frustrated, Genevieve turned to him in a huff. What could she do? It was her pride stinging most, nothing more. The outcome was what they'd hoped for. She should be thrilled. And there was still the matter of Orvis, not to mention fulfilling one more spot left open by Agatha. She had greater concerns than whether Mr. Kyi-yee wanted her present at the wedding. "I'm fine," she assured him. "Does Penelope know?"

Pastor Hammond smiled, appearing relieved. "Not yet. I thought I might let you share the happy news with her."

Confounded still by the odd request, Genevieve nodded, and pulled her shawl on around her shoulders. She stepped outside, hesitating as she scanned the street. Down the block, she spotted Penelope, head held high, her stride determined.

"Mrs. Jackson? Penelope?" Genevieve called as she lifted her skirts to follow.

The woman showed no signs of slowing.

"Penelope, may I speak with you?" Genevieve picked up her step, mentally reminding herself to speak with the mayor about installing better walkways on the main street. She noticed bits of straw on the back of Penelope's skirt. Why would she have been in the stables? Setting aside her curiosity, Genevieve hurried to catch up to her. "Penelope, wait. Please, I must speak with you."

Genevieve noted the curious onlookers—businesspeople, mostly, who she'd seen earlier whilst chasing Mr. Kyi-yee. If nothing else, she was certainly making a name for herself in this town as being tenacious. "Penny," she said, attempting to catch her breath after her swift walk down the main rough and slippery street.

Penelope stopped suddenly, but did not turn around immediately. Genevieve ascertained that she would have every right to be angry with her. She felt badly about how Silas had behaved and hoped her good news would be welcome.

"I have some wonderful news, Penny," Genevieve began, eying once more the straw covered bits on her skirt and jacket.

Penelope turned on her heel, startling Genevieve. Her gaze locked with Genevieve's, her eyes wide with a determination. She started to speak, then averted her eyes, her gaze coming to rest on her shoes. "Mrs. Walters… Genevieve. I was just on my way to La Maison…to lie down. I'm not feeling quite myself."

Genevieve's heart twisted. She could see how upset she was. She took her hand and squeezed it. "Penny, I know this day thus far has been dreadful and that you are thinking of giving up on the idea of marriage—perhaps altogether. But I beg you to listen to what I have to say."

The woman looked away. A wistful sigh preceded a sad smile. "You speak so highly of marriage, yet you choose to be alone. I can't help but wonder why."

Genevieve's heart faltered at the stark truth of her comment, the words striking too close, but as she'd done many times, she put her own needs aside. "Penelope, I know that you came to Noelle because I asked you to have faith—to try once more. I wouldn't blame you if you are angry with me."

Penny's soft gray eyes met hers. They were filled with kindness, but also, with resignation. "I bear no ill will toward you." She studied Genevieve. "It's simply that I don't feel I am meant for marriage."

Genevieve shook her head and squeezed Penny's hand. "That is not true. I have never known a woman more suited for marriage. You have so much to offer to the right man." She hoped her news would bring Penelope a change of heart. "Penelope, Pastor Hammond has found someone." Genevieve smiled. "He truly meets so many attributes that a woman desires in a good companion." In truth, she knew little about the man other than from an observational standpoint. "He appears to be well regarded here in Noelle. Friendly with most of the businessmen, seems to have a voracious appetite--"

"Mrs. Walters?" Penelope interrupted. "Can you not see that I am not meant to marry? Two of my husbands have died, a third has run off. Men cross the street when they see me. See if it's not true."

Genevieve looked over her shoulder and caught a trio of miners, chatting until they saw the two women. Glancing odd looks at them, the three crossed the street and resumed their walk to the Golden Nugget. "They were going to the saloon, Penelope."

The woman shook her head.

Genevieve persisted. "Miners are a suspicious lot. We both are well aware of this fact. This man is different. He doesn't work for the mine. He is self-made. Strong. Resilient."

Penelope's gaze focused on a group of men who'd just come out of the Nugget. They'd stopped to chat, and, given the glances cast their way, it was likely that the topic was about Silas's sudden departure. It was a small town. News traveled fast.

"If he isn't superstitious, then he must not be from around here," Penny commented, returning her attention to Genevieve.

It was a crumb. Not much, but enough for Genevieve to work with. If nothing else, she wasn't entirely disinterested. "If ever there was a man on the face of this earth who needed the gentle care and companionship of the right woman—that being you—it is this man they call Kyi-yee."

Penny's eyes darted to hers. A flicker of concern crossed her face. "Does he even speak English, Mrs. Walters?"

Genevieve nodded. "He came from the East with his brother three years ago. His brother was killed in a mining accident—tragic, really. He wandered then at some length, and when he was attacked by a grizzly and survived, the local Indians took him in and nursed him back to health. Because he survived, they gave him the name Kyi-yee, which means 'bear'." Genevieve hurried on before Penelope could ask questions that she could not answer. She wasn't aware of what physical scars the man might carry from the attack, but she prayed that Penelope would have the constitution to look beyond the scars to the man. "He has since acted to protect the town from predators as he is an excellent hunter and also serves as liaison between the Indians and the town during times of great tension. He is fearless it seems, but a good provider. I doubt you would ever want for anything. He trades his pelts in town in exchange for goods, providing the means for the people here to have warm boots, blankets, jackets. It's no wonder he is regarded so highly around here."

Penelope's lackluster eyes looked at Genevieve. There was no joy embedded in her expression; simply a dull apathy. "He sounds fine enough."

Fueled by hope, Genevieve continued with more enthusiasm. "Pastor Hammond has spoken to him and he has told him he wishes to marry you. He knows nothing of your past. Here is a man you could build a good future with and I am certain," she added with a smile, "that beneath all of those pelts and…well, hair…walks a man who is undoubtedly handsome." She might have gone on about the strength of his muscular thighs, but she chose to keep that to herself. Besides, if Penny agreed, she would see for herself soon enough.

Penny looked off into the distance. "I admit he sounds too wonderful, nearly out of a dream. In fact, the manner in which you speak of him gives the inclination that he is more suited to you, Genevieve."

She was taken aback. "Surely, you jest," she said. "May I remind you that I have a life, a position at the mission back in Denver. And the success of this endeavor and my part in it, is being watched carefully by my superiors—most of them men who had little faith that we would even survive the train. See what we've accomplished already? There are only two days left until the obligation with the railroad is to be met. Remember, that is our goal. Our sole purpose in traveling all this way."

"Is that all this is to you, then? A job? An obligation? How can you know what will make others happy if you deny happiness yourself?"

Penelope's point was well taken, however misguided it was. Genevieve turned the woman's face to hers, meeting her eye-to-eye. "I have experienced marriage in my life. I have known what love is, what responsibility and companionship is. I have also known loss. And that is why I feel called, you see, to help others find the happiness I've known." She forced a smile, realizing that her tale was not entirely true. Her marriage had been brief, their time together cut short by the responsibilities of war. But her heart had been known to flutter seeing him in his uniform, sitting grand upon his horse. Their last kiss, though chaste, was infused with her need to be strong for him. Genevieve dropped her gaze, her face warming to another time, to when the stolen kiss of a young soldier caused her body to stir in ways unimaginable.

"If you had loved once, it would seem that you would desire to find such love again. I know I would."

"Yes," Genevieve said. "That is precisely what I am asking…don't give up. Give this man a chance."

Resignation painted her small smile.

"Pastor Hammond is speaking with Mr. Malone even as we speak, making the arrangements for the ceremony this evening. As you are aware, the vows must be completed in twelve days of our arrival according to the agreement with the railroad. This may well be your perfect match, Penelope. I beseech you reconsider."

Penelope seemed faraway in her thoughts.

Genevieve touched her shoulder. "Come a little early, say eleven. and at least meet the man. You can then judge for yourself whether Mr. Kyi-Yee is suited to you."

Penelope offered a weary sigh. "If you'll excuse me. I need to rest." She lifted her skirts and turned to walk towards La Maison.

Genevieve clasped her hands to her chin and watched her leave, compelled to offer one last vote of confidence for the potential groom. "Did I mention what a fine physique he has?" *And the bluest eyes.* "I'm sure he'd appreciate a woman who loves adventure." *And doesn't mind living in a cabin in the mountains.* "Who loves to cook as much as you do!" she called at the top of her voice. *And hopefully you have recipes for bear meat.*

Genevieve shaded her eyes to the shaft of sunlight beaming straight down from overhead. It was only noon. She sighed. With any luck, Penelope might feel entirely different after she rested. That was her hope. And with that hope, she turned on her heel to find Birdie and retrieve the veil she'd made for Penny. Besides, she might need to enlist Birdie's help in convincing her friend to marry tonight.

She walked out into the street, feeling the warmth of the sun, however fleeting before the gray clouds overcame its brilliance. She would take it as a sign from above that all would be well and that, with a little rest and a smidge of divine intervention, Penelope would see the God's open door had provided a man far better than Silas.

Chapter Ten

"You're a damn fool," Zeke muttered to himself as he pulled his sled up the steep trail he and Clem had once blazed up the mountainside. The ache in his chest reminded him how unfair it was to marry one woman when his heart belonged still to another. But for her happiness, he would go through the ceremony at least. The union might last, it might not. Once she saw the scars left on his body, she'd likely leave just as his first wife had done.

He tied the horse in the barn and stoking a roaring fire in the cabin, dragged the copper tub close to the stone fireplace. Using a yoke fashioned with two buckets balanced over his shoulders, he walked a few yards from his home and using a pick ax broke the ice enough to gather in three trips enough water to fill the tub halfway.

He dropped his jacket over a rack made of deer antlers and unlacing his boots, skimmed down to his long underwear. Testing the water, it was still too chilly for his tastes, so he sat down at his small dining table with one chair and scanned the room, regret of his choice beginning to swell inside him as he thought of what type of home he had to offer a new bride.

There was nothing feminine--no lace, no gingham curtains, none of the finery a woman from the cities back East would consider proper.

Everything had been crafted with function in mind. The furnishings were simple. There was a large bed that he and his brother had shared until they could build a bigger cabin. It was made with wood and rope, its mattress stuffed with straw. There was a table and only one chair now. Zeke had burnt the other in an emotional rage after his brother died. Then came the bear attack.

His recovery from that was more of a blur. He'd determined later that he'd spent several months in the Ute camp under the watchful eye of an old Indian—one of the elders who had been asked to leave by the government, but returned to live out his days in the only place he'd ever known as home. Given what Zeke saw with the aid of a broken piece of mirror he had been lucky to survive. It had taken him days to get the strength to stand, longer still until he'd made a full recovery.

He'd bonded as a son to the Native American elder and had learned much about surviving the wilderness. In the process of recovery, he'd learned how unfair the government had been in their desire to acquire the land and the gold believed to be on it.

He'd shied away from people, living off the land, becoming an expert hunter, and fishing with a spear—sometimes with his bare hands. After the attack, he'd found that soaking in a warm spring eased the sensitivity of the formation of new skin and his nerve endings reconnecting. But when the weather turned, it became apparent he'd need a tub of his own. And after the reaction of his former bride, the thought of bathing in a public place was out of the question.

It had been Culver at the blacksmith shop who'd suggested a place that made copper tubs, and he'd offered his wagon and assistance in hauling the tub. He was the first white man Zeke had spoken to since the bear attack and, once the flood gates opened, Zeke had found himself pouring out to the rough-looking blacksmith everything from his guilt about his brother to the grizzly attack and so, too, the bride who'd rejected him because of it. Culver had been the first person he'd ever spoken to about his personal demons.

And the last.

Forcing himself from his reverie, Zeke gathered his shaving supplies, including a small mirror he'd traded for in town and set them beside the tub. Dipping his hand in the water, he checked to make sure the warmth of the fire had succeeded in making the water tepid enough to tolerate.

He undressed, aware of the places where his muscles ached deep. Easing into the tub, he winced as the now-tepid water enveloped him. The heat from the fire helped some. He leaned his head against the edge of the copper tub and, closing his eyes, let go the notion that he was making a mistake even as the memory of the first day he'd met Genevieve Walters slipped into his thoughts.

***

Weary from riding, Zeke slid off his horse and dropped the reins. For a moment, he stood and took in the lush, green spans of lawn around him. It felt as though his lungs were caked in gun smoke. He closed his eyes, breathing deep the fresh air, grateful for the scent of lilacs in bloom instead of the stench of death.

He looked at the stately home before him--a mansion in comparison to the simple clapboard farm house in which he grew up. The graceful three-story home with its gabled turret was painted a pristine white. Same color porch posts, gingerbread and lattice, decorated the porch that wrapped around three sides. A wooden swing anchored one end of the porch overlooked a row of short lilacs bushes in a welcoming fashion.

Zeke fought the urge to drop to his knees and kiss the earth. Remembering his purpose, the woman he'd come to see, he forced his feet to climb the steps to the front door.

An odd mix of fear and anticipation caused him to hesitate before knocking. It was a late May afternoon. The slow buzz of crickets filled the air. He knocked. The front door opened. And there she stood--the embodiment of the hope and tenderness he'd come to know through the letters she'd written to her husband, giving him the will to survive the horrors of war. And she didn't even know his name. Zeke found his tongue, her beauty threatening to scatter his reason to the four winds.

"My name is Sergeant Christian Ezekiel Kinnison, ma'am. Good day. I'm here on personal business for Mrs. Walters." He was certain he'd stuttered and remembering his hat, yanked it from his head.

Her expression was pensive as she assessed him. Still there was kindness in her thoughtful gaze. "Are you looking for my mother-in-law or me, sir?"

Pulling himself from from the reverie of his lovesick thoughts, he averted his eyes, looking instead at his tattered boots, mentally scolding himself as a reminder of why he was there. His heart pounded in his chest. The news he'd been trusted to deliver now sat like boulders around his neck. He could not bear to see this woman in pain "Are you…Genevieve?" He pulled his gaze to hers and her hand flew to her heart.

She knew.

"I am Genevieve Walters," she said in a hushed voice.

"Perhaps, ma'am, we should sit," he suggested.

Another woman, older, appeared behind her. Her expression was curious until Zeke realized she'd taken in his Union uniform.

"Is it Levi?" Her question held fear and resignation. Many families would be feeling the same in the days ahead as the ravages of war became clear.

A lump formed in his throat as he stared at the two faces willing him not to speak the dreaded words. "It is my duty to inform you"--he stumbled over the words, emotion making it difficult to speak--"that Captain Walters succumbed to injuries received while serving in battle."

Zeke watched as the blood drained from the elderly woman's face. Her knees buckled and he lunged forward catching her before she crumbled to the ground. He carried her limp body to the parlor, where an older man and woman appeared from another door assisting him as he eased her to the parlor sofa.

He stepped away to address the young woman he'd left in shock. He'd seen her photograph only once carried in the frame of his captain's watch fob. He pulled out the watch and a bundle of letters, both of which he'd promised his superior to return to his wife should the unthinkable ever happen. Zeke never expected to be standing here.

"Did he know the war had ended? That the Union won?"

Zeke paused, debating how to answer. He'd not been at his captain's side, but had made his way to the infirmary as planned the moment a messenger had informed him of his passing. "I'm not certain that he was aware the battle had officially ended." He looked at his tattered, worn boots, thought of the men—young and old—he'd seen lying dead on a string of open fields. "I don't know that it's possible to say there was a victory, ma'am." He met her narrow gaze. "My apologies. I should keep my thoughts private."

"No, please. Share them. I know the ideals my husband fought and died for, sir. What is it you fought for?" There was a measure of anger mixed with grief in her voice.

He paused to consider her question. "I fought, as many did, for the ideals which Captain Walters believed in, ma'am." He shook his head. "But the cost of preserving those ideals has come with a heavy toll--to families, to children who will never have fathers, to mothers who have lost their children, the toll of what I've seen--" He stopped and sighed. His soul weighed with weariness and sorrow. "The loss is high. I only hope we can retain those ideals for which so much blood has been shed."

Her frustration seemed to subside. She regarded him with a kindness that soothed his soul and, at the same time, riddled him with guilt. "Forgive me, Sergeant Kinnison, I meant no disrespect. I thank you for your service and continue to believe that one day all men…and women will be of equal importance in this world."

When the elder Mrs. Walters had recovered from her fainting spell, she'd graciously asked him to dine and recuperate before he began his journey home. Zeke had agreed, but his motives were anything but chaste. He'd been the right arm of his captain, gained his explicit trust, and had been given the privilege of reading each and every one of his wife's letters aloud to his war-weary superior. And in doing so, he'd fallen in love with the woman in those letters. Which is why it was important that he keep his distance from her.

"Sergeant Kinnison, what are your plans now?" the elder Mrs. Walters asked him at supper the next night. He'd been given other clothes to wear during his stay so that his uniform might be cleaned. He shifted uncomfortably in the trousers and jacket that fit a trifle snug on his broad shoulders. He dabbed his mouth with his napkin before he spoke. His gaze met Genevieve's emerald green eyes across the table and, though he hadn't purposely kept count, he'd noticed a number of her stolen glances.

"My brother and I have plans to go west." The thought of his brother, his excitement to explore the new frontier, brought a smile to his face. "He feels we should be among those to stake our claim in the West." He snorted softly. "I believe he's been taken in by claims of gold in the mountains."

Genevieve smiled. Zeke could not take his eyes off her.

"Yet, Mr. Kinnison, you do not share the same interest as your brother?"

He regarded her before he spoke. "Perhaps it is battle that gives a man clarity, Mrs. Walters. I am not entranced by the glint of gold." He glanced at his plate—fine china, silver utensils, and crystal goblets. They were all very nice, but nothing like his farm upbringing. "I am a simple man." He scanned the room before meeting the gazes of his two dining companions.

"I look around at your lovely home, with a warm fire in the hearth, food on the table, seeing the generosity and kindness among those who live here—that, along with a beautiful, devoted woman that Captain Walters was fortunate enough to call his wife—it is my belief that he was one of the wealthiest men I've ever known."

Genevieve held his gaze, though he noted the faint blush at his complimentary description. She blinked and suddenly averted her gaze.

"You are a gracious young man," said the older Mrs. Walters. "My husband, rest his soul, poured everything he had into this land. He was son to immigrants and they had to fashion a life on their own. It is my belief that good men understand the importance of hearth and home."

Her words touched him. "I have seen the best in a man and his worst. It has led me to believe that our Creator had more in mind than the destruction brought about by misperceptions of our fellow man." A quiet sigh escaped his lips. "Freedom, I surmise, is not given freely. There is always, sadly, it seems, a price."

Wishing to turn the conversation to more pleasant topics, Zeke looked at the woman who by right, owned this house and its land. "Have you plans to stay on and carry on your husband's work, ma'am?"

The older woman shook her head. "We'd planned on Levi and Genevieve to take over and carry on." She hesitated and glanced at her daughter-in-law. "I have a brother in Denver, who has invited us to come live with him and his wife. He has grave concerns of us living alone—just the two of us." She smiled at Genevieve. "Perhaps it is best we now consider his offer with greater seriousness."

Chapter Eleven

Genevieve stared at the small blue flower painted on the teacup Birdie had given her. She thought of the strange mountain man with eyes the color of a summer sky.

"Mrs. Walters?"

Birdie's voice pulled her from her thoughts. She realized she'd been day-dreaming, prompted, by the disturbing--yet revealing--conversation with Penelope.

"My apologies Birdie. I fear my thoughts are a bit scattered."

"Has there been word of Silas's return?" Birdie asked, placing the tissue-wrapped veil on the table.

"I'm afraid not, but Pastor Hammond and I have found another man who has agreed to marry Penelope."

Birdie nearly choked on her tea. "From Noelle?" she asked in surprise.

"Not exactly. It is my understanding that he and his brother came to Noelle shortly after the mine opened. There was a tragic accident—though I am not aware of all the details—but, sadly his brother was killed."

Birdie's hand flew to her chest. *"Que horreur!"*

"This man apparently retreated into the mountains and somehow survived an attack by a grizzly bear."

Birdie looked at Genevieve with concern. "Mrs. Walters, from what I know about Penny she is a most understanding woman, but under present circumstances should we expect more from her?"

Noting her concern, Genevieve sighed. "I have thought of that, yes, but she is here, and her purpose in coming was to marry. No, he's not written the flowery letters she received from Silas, that is true. But something in this man's persona, in how he treats others, what good the pastor says he's done for the people here makes me feel he may well be a far better match for Penny."

Genevieve hurried on, caught up in finding a way to explain what perfect marriage partners the two would be. "Penny is independent, but has a gentle side that this man most certainly needs. Penny could use a man who believes in her, cherishes her."

"And you believe after just a few hours that this man is her best match," Birdie eyed Genevieve.

"I know this," Genevieve straightened her shoulders. "I can attest he is quite a handsome man under his substantial beard and quite a healthy head of hair. And he has the most remarkable blue eyes—why if I were looking for a husband myself--which I am not--he would most certainly qualify as a candidate." Genevieve caught the curious look on Birdie's face and stopped. "And to be certain, I spoke with him personally and found him to be a most suitable groom—broad shoulders, kind, self-sufficient, diplomatic."

Birdie smiled. "Well, that should come in handy in the bedroom. Has Penelope met him? Does he have a name?"

"The townsfolk call him Kyi-yee—it was given to him by the Indian who found him after the attack. I'm told that he was under his care for quite some time, that he almost died. He became friends and has on occasion acted as a buffer between the townspeople and Indians when tensions arise."

"But you haven't answered my other question. Has Penelope met him?" Birdie asked.

Genevieve took a sip of tea averting Birdie's questioning look. "Not yet. But I'm hoping once she has rested, she will agree to meet him at the saloon. I'm sure once she does, she will be as taken as I am." Genevieve took out her pocket watch and realized that two hours had passed since she'd left Penelope. "Thank you, kindly for the tea." She picked up the wrapped veil "Oh, and if it isn't a great imposition, might I ask you and your husband to stand in as witnesses this evening? I think it would put Penelope at ease to know she was among someone she trusts."

"Certainly," she said, though obviously perplexed. "I assume you will also be there?"

Genevieve wrapped her shawl around her shoulders, preparing for the walk back to La Maison at the other end of town. She held the tissue bundle beneath her shawl to protect it. "That is a bit of a conundrum, I'm afraid. It seems that Mr. Kyi-yee, while willing to marry Penelope, has imposed on Pastor Hammond a single request."

Birdie frowned. "And what is that?"

She dismissed the annoying request with a sigh. "It seems Mr. Kyi-yee does not wish *me* present at the ceremony."

Birdie opened her mouth to speak. Genevieve stopped her with an upturned hand. "Pastor reminded me it is for the greater good and I have to agree. Our primary purpose here is to give Penelope a good husband and hope for happiness."

"Doesn't that seem odd?" Birdie asked.

Genevieve nodded "I would agree. And I hope that I may yet convince Mr. Kyi-yee to have a change of heart on the matter." She lifted her shoulder. "But we must do what is best to fulfill our agreement and save Noelle."

"And make certain Penelope finds happiness," Birdie interjected.

"That, without question," Genevieve said, "is paramount." She shook her head. "Since Agatha chose to join Madame at La Maison, I must go to see if I can convince her to reconsider. On that topic, I understand that your new father-in-law is unattached?"

Birdie's eyes flew open at the suggestion, and a curious look flickered through them.

"I imagine a newly married couple getting to know each other, might enjoy some help with a man like Gus? Perhaps a bride?"

"Oh, Mrs. Walters, I'm not certain my husband would agree."

"Perhaps there'd be no harm in at least offering the idea?" Genevieve asked. "We could discuss it further this evening at the saloon?"

"I make no promises, Mrs. Walters on the subject of Agatha. But I believe I can get him to agree to be witness for the ceremony this evening."

"Splendid! I thank you for being such a good friend to Penelope." Genevieve's smile wobbled. "You all will need each other after I return to Denver." She sniffed, shaking her head to balance her emotions. "I must go. Eleven o'clock at the Nugget."

***

Genevieve marveled at Pastor Hammond's words—when God closes one door, he opens another. Doubtful that she'd find the passage in the Good Book, she had been witness to its truth more than once today. She had only to speak to Agatha and hope that Penelope's rest had given her a renewed sense of hope.

Penelope's bedroom door was closed. Genevieve lifted her fist, debating whether to knock. She glanced at her husband's watch and after the chaos of the day decided a few more minutes of rest wouldn't hurt Penny, or her.

She walked into the front parlor, its plush furnishings oddly out of place in the ramshackle town. Red velvet curtains with gold tassels separated the room from the foyer. Here, Genevieve surmised, was where men could be entertained with food and drink as they awaited a woman chosen for their needs. Rich floral and velvet fabrics covered the settees and Queen Anne chairs. Gilded mirrors hung on the walls, a player piano stood in one corner.

Drawn to a gentler time when she played piano in the evenings, Genevieve sat on the tufted piano stool. She ran her fingers over the worn keys. The delicate sound echoed in the empty house. The events of the morning, Penny's challenging admonition, Seamus's desire to rekindle his marriage, and Orvis asking her help with Miss Boum Boum—it all seemed to converge on her heart at once. Emotions she'd fought to set aside, desires she'd long ago tried to bury in her work surfaced. Memories of a young soldier with the bluest eyes she'd ever gazed into, the low-timbred voice that comforted her grieving heart the secret confession he'd shared with her in the moonlight in the veranda that fateful night…

With one hand she plucked out the notes of the song she'd tried hard to forget--the tune the young soldier had played on his mouth pipe. *Beautiful Dreamer*.

***

"It is my duty to inform you"--the young soldier dressed in his tattered Union uniform stumbled—"to inform you that Captain Walters succumbed to injuries received while serving in battle."

Frozen in place, Genevieve saw his lips moving but not until the officer stepped forward to catch her mother-in-law did she realize the woman had been standing beside her, receiving the dreadful news at the same time.

She pointed him to the parlor where two of the estate staff--an old married couple who had despite the emancipation setting them free, chose to remain after the elder Mr. Walters had passed—aided him in settling her onto the sofa.

Reeling still from the news, Genevieve stood motionless in the door to the parlor digesting the surreal news that she'd just become a widow.

***

The sound of a door slamming upstairs jarred Genevieve from her thoughts. She walked to the stairway to see if Penelope had woken from her rest. Instead she found Agatha.

"Good day, Mrs. Walters." Agatha said. She was dressed in her finest dress of calico and lace.

Genevieve stood at the bottom of the staircase, her hand on the railing. "My, Agatha, but don't you look fetching this fine afternoon. Special plans?" Genevieve asked.

Agatha lowered her voice as she descended the steps. "I have a beau," she said primly.

"A beau? Who pray tell?" Genevieve tried not to sound too exuberant about the prospect that her absentee twelfth bride might still be resolved.

"It's a young man who comes to see me three times a week. He carves these tiny animals. Brings a new one each time he visits."

"Does Madame allow these gifts?"

Agatha's eyes twinkled. "What she don't know won't hurt her. Besides, he pays, so she gets her cut."

"And he's a nice man? One you feel safe with? Easy to talk to? Does he have your best interest at heart?" Genevieve was intrigued. Perhaps there was hope yet that Noelle could be saved.

Agatha raised her brows. "That's a lot of territory to cover in less than a week, Mrs. Walters. But he is a gentleman. Pays for services and then we sit and talk the whole time. He is a very learned man."

"Why Agatha, he sounds wonderful. Is he…young enough for you?" Genevieve skirted around the topic. She'd never met a woman with Agatha's constitution at her age.

"You mean do I find him compatible in all ways?" she asked with a sly grin. "We haven't gotten around to that just yet. He keeps forgetting why he shows up at the house and so we just talk. But from what I can determine, it appears everything is in tip-top shape."

"This is wonderful news," Genevieve said. "Do you suppose a consideration of marriage is possible?"

Agatha seemed to chew on the thought. "Oh, I suppose it's possible." She shrugged then smiled sweetly. "He is a dear man. Did I mention he brings me these tiny animals he's carved?"

Gus? Genevieve smiled, believing more and more in Pastor Hammond's belief about doors opening. "You did, actually, yes. I think it's wonderful."

Agatha's eyes darted to Genevieve. "But you mustn't breathe a word of this to anyone. No one, not even his grandson, knows about us."

"You have my word," Genevieve said.

"Marriage, hum…" Agatha grinned. "No promises, Mrs. Walters. Want to get to know this one a bit first. Still, the thought isn't entirely terrible."

Genevieve nodded. Her heart pleased that Agatha had found someone it seemed she enjoyed being with. What more could she ask than that? "Oh, by the way, have you seen Penelope Jackson?"

Agatha paused, her hand on the doorknob. "Earlier, she had a bag. Looked like she was moving out."

Confused, Genevieve looked on as Agatha turned to grab her shawl from the hall tree. "I told that Madame Bon—whatever her name is—that I wanted to live in this house and I would come over in the evenings. To be fair, I haven't much liked what I've seen over there and I'm just as happy for Gus's company. That sorry excuse for a woman doesn't treat her ladies very kindly. And I don't take kindly to bullies."

She was still pondering if the woman Agatha saw was Penny. She might have been mistaken. "Agatha, I think you're right to feel as you do about Madame Bonheur. Be careful of her."

"Yes, ma'am, I will." Agatha grinned. She was even at seventy a lovely woman with silvery hair worn in a braided bun atop her head. Her eyes, bright blue sparkled with mischief. She and Gus would most certainly make a handsome couple, should they ever choose marriage as an option

Genevieve stopped Agatha before she left. "Are you certain it was Penelope you saw? She indicated to me she needed to rest. Why would she just decide—" the sudden realization that Penny may have left town completely pushed Genevieve up the stairs.

Finding the door closed, Genevieve knocked once, then opened the door. The room was void of anyone still residing there. Penelope's bag was indeed gone. Propped on the dresser was a white envelope. Genevieve saw her name written neatly across the paper. She removed the folded notepaper inside, her eyes blurring as she read Penelope's words.

Dear Genevieve,

My heart is heavy as I write this, knowing how reading it will hurt you; yet I must be true to my convictions and not allow weakness to dissuade me. You have been true and faithful, and have always had my fulfillment as your highest priority, and for that I cannot find words to express my gratitude. But Providence has made it clear to me, and now I must accept, that marriage is not meant to be my future.

By the time you read this, I will have left town. Now, I am leaving to go see Mr. Hardt about arranging to take me to the depot, and will be catching the first train back to Denver in the morning. We can correspond once I'm settled. I shall look forward to hearing more about this man you

believe represents the best possible husband material. If he is as wonderful as you say he is, then I think you should consider him for yourself.

You spoke to us ladies often of the deep and abiding happiness that can be found in a loving companionship, so I implore you to embrace the opportunity to find your own happiness. Search your heart, dear friend. It will not lead you astray.

Most affectionately yours,

Penny

Genevieve brushed a tear from her cheek, tucked the note into her pocket, and hurried downstairs. Retrieving her shawl, she opened the front door and let out a startled yelp.

"I have *zomething* I *weesh* to speak with you about *Meesus* Walters." Madame Bonheur walked past Genevieve, her skirts whooshing as she turned to face her. "It has come to my *attencion* that you are attempting to sabotage my business."

Genevieve stood, her hand in her pocket, debating how she could defuse Madame's anger as quickly as possible. It was imperative she find Penelope. "Madame Bonheur, I implore you. Can this wait? I have more pressing matters--"

"Do you not *theenk* that my livelihood, the welfare of my girls is not of grave importance?" she bellowed.

Genevieve's ire rose along with the woman's voice. "Madame Bonheur—if that is indeed your real name, for you are no more French than I am a saloon girl. I must attend to my own matters."

Madame reared back as though Genevieve had slapped her. She held up her finger. "YOU have been trying to get my Boum Boum to leave me."

"*Your* Boum Boum?" Genevieve was in no mood to take Madame's accusations. "Do you think then that you own her, as though she were an animal, or here to serve your bidding?"

Madame's eyes widened. "I warn you, Mrs. Walters. I don't give a damn about your *leetle tête-à-tête* with the mayor or the preacher. It is my business that has kept this town from going under." She slapped her fist to her ample breasts. "Ever since you arrived you have created chaos for me. First my Pearl leaves, buying into your silly notions for marriage."

"Pearl? You are most certainly misguided or that tight corset had blocked the blood flow to your brain since I have neither the time or interest in your cushy little business. And your thoughts on the railroad agreement and how it may or may not affect you is a matter you will have to take up with Mayor Hardt—your landlord, so I understand." Genevieve leveled a look at the woman she'd just about had enough of. "And perhaps he'd be interested to know how poorly you treat the women who work at La Maison."

Madame gasped and covered her mouth.

Genevieve took a step toward the shocked woman. "As far as Miss Boum Boum, or Pearl, or any of the women of La Maison"--Genevieve waved her hand as her voice rose in ire—"any whorehouse from here to either coast. "I would most ardently defend her right—or any woman, for that matter the right to make her own choices," Genevieve countered.

Madame shoved her finger beneath Genevieve's nose. "Then you admit to you encouraged Orvis Weston to abscond with my Boum Boum ?" It was peculiar though not entirely surprising that Madame's French accent had faded away, a richer, nasal tone taking its place along with her anger.

Genevieve squared her shoulders and held Madame's steely gaze "If they love each other, then I do not see why anyone or anything should stand in the way of their happiness She prayed the woman did not carry a small pistol under her skirts as many women in her profession did.

"Love? What makes you think Boum Boum knows anything about love? Or worse, that low-life of a man, Orvis Weston? He's nothing but a filthy miner who will never have more than the shirt on his back!"

Genevieve studied her, then shook her head. "I feel sorry for you Madame Bonheur. For as enterprising as you believe yourself to be, you really have no idea how to treat others with a decency and respect. I wonder is it because you were once treated so poorly that you feel others should share in your pain? Wake up, Madame Bonheur. There is a new day dawning where women will share a greater respect for themselves. They will see the value in who they are and in the choices they make. If you do not change, you will remain enslaved in your own bitterness."

The sound of a man clearing his throat brought both women's heads around to the open front door. Orvis and Miss Boum Boum stood just outside. Considering the shocked expression on both of their faces it appeared they'd heard much of the conversation.

"I must be going." Genevieve glanced at Madame. "And you, it seems have some explaining to do to these good people. Good day," she said, stepping past the couple in the door. She touched Boum Boum's arm. "If you wish my help or should you require Pastor Hammond's services, they are both yours." She smiled and hurried up the street to find the preacher.

Genevieve was walking past the diner and nearly ran into Woody Burnside as he left it. He caught Genevieve's arms to steady her from falling.

"Mrs. Walters, pardon ma'am, you look white as a sheet. Are you well?" Woody asked.

Taking a cleansing breath, she looked at Woody. Here was a man who was well versed in Noelle's comings and goings.

"It's about one of my ladies," she began.

Woody's gaze narrowed. "Mrs. Jackson?"

Surprised, Genevieve nodded. "Have you seen her?"

Woody nodded and scratched his chin in thought. "Oh yes, ma'am. She told me her plans earlier when she came by the barn looking to leave. I sent her to Mr. Hardt."

Genevieve's shoulders felt as though she carried an ox yoke. "You're certain it was her?"

"Oh, yes, ma'am. She bid me goodbye."

Genevieve turned away, her hand to her forehead as the fate of not only Noelle, but now Penny, weighed heavily on her mind.

"Is there anything I can do, ma'am?" he asked.

She looked over her shoulder. "If you could find Pastor Hammond and explain what you've told me. Tell him I'm going to notify Mr. Kyi-yee of the situation and that I will speak with him upon my return."

Woody nodded. "Yes, ma'am. Are you sure you wouldn't like for me to go with you to speak to Kyi-yee?"

She darted him a look. "Should I be concerned for my well-being?"

"No ma'am. Nothing at all like that. Kyi-yee is one of the finest men I know. It's just…well, ma'am it is some ways by horse up into the mountains. You not being familiar with the trail and all."

"Thank you for your concern, Mr. Burnside. I'll be fine, and will be back in short order. If you might find Pastor Hammond."

Woody nodded and Genevieve walked up the street toward Culver's Livery and Blacksmith.

Culver Daniels eyed Genevieve as she strode toward him. He lay down his hammer and wiped his blackened hands on his apron.

"Mrs. Walters?"

"Mr. Daniels. I am in need of a horse," she stated. "I have no purse with me at the present, but I presume my reputation is good for payment for an hour or two?"

He nodded. "Certainly, ma'am." He glanced at her, then over her shoulders. "Will it be just you then?"

"Yes, sir."

He nodded again, but hesitated.

"You're curious as to why I would need a horse, Mr. Daniels?

"Well, it's not a day suited for pleasure riding." He glanced up at the gloomy winter sky. "These horses are my living, Mrs. Walters. Seems my right to know where you plan to ride."

"Fair enough. I need to ride up to pay a visit to Mr. Kyi-yee."

Culver frowned, then he gave her an incredulous look. "Mister? I've always just called him Kyi-yee."

"Very well, then. Kyi-yee." She stomped past him and bee-lined for the stables behind the blacksmith shop. It didn't take long for Culver to match her pace.

"I heard that he told Pastor Hammond he'd marry Mrs. Jackson."

Genevieve stopped and faced him. "How did you—? Never mind." She dismissed her question. Small town. She doubted she needed Woody to find the preacher. Someone had probably already informed him of her plans.

"You know, I have to say I'm a bit surprised."

"And why is that, Mr. Daniels?" Genevieve was in a hurry. She needed to break the news to the man who'd suffered so much already in his life. She wasn't looking forward to being the bearer of bad news, but perhaps if he were willing they could yet need his help if she could find the right woman. Which likely meant cajoling Madame, yet again.

"You're aware he lost his brother?" Culver said.

Genevieve nodded. "Pastor Hammond shared that tragic story with me, yes. How about the palomino? He looks gentle." Genevieve pointed to the smaller of the horses stabled.

"Buttercup is gentle. Good choice." Culver began to saddle the horse. "And you're aware of the grizzly attack—since you know he's gone by Kyi-yee instead of his real name since?"

Genevieve scratched the muzzle of the horse as she waited. "His real name? Pastor Hammond didn't know what it was…do you?"

Culver cinched the stirrup straps in place. "Goes by Zeke, ma'am."

"Zeke, hmm," she commented, maneuvering so that Mr. Daniels could give her a leg up mounting the horse.

"I have to tell you I was pleased to hear that he'd even agree to marry again after his experience with that bride."

"Bride? Kyi-yee, er…Zeke is married?" Genevieve came to a startling realization. "Oh heavens! Is the poor man a widow? No wonder he was so shy about talking with me. His grief must be immeasurable!"

The burly blacksmith eyed her with a frown. "No, ma'am. That wedding was annulled within a week. The way Kyi-yee told it, she was scared off by the scars."

"From the bear attack." Genevieve's heart softened for the man. "Oh, how unfortunate. No wonder he lives like a hermit up on the mountain."

Culver smiled. "Just him and that dern harmonica of his. He never goes anywhere without it."

Genevieve's gaze whipped to the blacksmith. *What were the odds? There could be hundreds…thousands of men with eyes that blue who play the harmonica, who had headed out west with his brother.*

"Is he any good?" she asked. Every nerve in her body came alert to the very idea that she might have been standing in front of the soldier she'd once kissed and had dreamt of for years after.

Culver nodded. "Pretty good. Has a favorite though. Said it got him through some difficult times--"

"In the war," Genevieve finished without thinking. "*Beautiful Dreamer.*"

Culver looked at her in surprise. "Why, yes, that's what he told me. Didn't know Zeke had mentioned that to anyone else."

"Zeke…short for Ezekiel." Genevieve held Culver's curious gaze. "His last name wouldn't happen to be *Kinnison*?"

"Why, yes, ma'am. Before the bear attack. He and his brother Clem--"

"Thank you, Mr. Culver." Bringing the horse around Genevieve nudged its sides and took off down the main street toward the trail on the other side of town that lead to the elusive mountain man's home. She was certain that she'd left Mr. Daniels thoroughly confused.

But certainly, no more than she felt.

A small log cabin appeared in a small grove of trees. A barn with a corral big enough for one horse stood off to one side. A rooster and a few hens scattered across the yard as she approached. No one appeared to be home, but smoke curled from the chimney. She climbed down from the horse and tied her to the rail outside. She walked up the single step to the porch and mustering her courage stood, debating whether to knock or leave and let the past remain in the past.

Chapter Twelve

A snap of a log brought Zeke out of a deep sleep. His chest ached at the memory of Genevieve's face, how he'd felt helpless. How he'd wished he could have taken away her pain. He'd felt the guilt of being the messenger of death—but *her* pain was his. In every letter she'd written her husband, he'd been the one to read them. Every tender word, every heartfelt sentence he came to cherish and adore. He'd started to look forward to her letters, perhaps more than her husband had. And Zeke had made the promise should anything happen to his captain that he would return his belongings, including those letters.

He'd done what he had been asked of him, but the stolen kiss they'd shared he'd shoved deep in the back of his mind. But in all these years, the memory of her mouth on his, the taste of her lips, could still cause his body to burn. Even now, he remembered seeing her, wanting to take her in his arms, tell her that he'd be there for her always if she wanted. But the guilt of loving her was too powerful, his loyalty to his captain unwavering.

How in God's name could he marry another woman when the one he'd be thinking of was Genevieve?

***

After dinner, Zeke had retreated outside to the shadows of the porch, hoping that physically distancing himself would quell this forbidden yearning he carried inside for Genevieve Walters every time their eyes met.

Softly, he played his harmonica, the melodies soothing the desires raging inside him. It would've been wiser to leave, not tempting fate by staying one night in this house with her.

The screen door opened. He stopped playing.

"I thought I heard music out here. Please don't let me stop you. It's been ages since I've heard such a sweet melody." She held a post as she sat perched on the porch rail. The simple act, tugged the cotton bodice of her dress tight, outlining the gentle curve of her breasts. He swallowed forcing his gaze to her face.

"It's a lovely tune. What is it?" she asked.

Zeke licked his lips, unable to stop staring at how the moon illuminated her face—the gentle slope of her neck. She wore her dark hair swept up off her neck and he could only imagine how it might feel to run his fingers through it, watch it tumble from its perfection into a wild tangle.

The song. Zeke looked away to gather his thoughts. *"Beautiful Dreamer.* The men found it calming after a hard day" --he hesitated—"in battle." He tapped his harmonica against his knee. "Sorry, ma'am. I'm sure you'd rather not hear about the war."

She'd looked at him her head tipped as though she were debating what to think. "Would you play some more? For me?"

Zeke's heart swelled with pride. He wanted to tell her that he'd cross a trail of fire for her, but things were what they were. She was a new widow. Had to have time to grieve her late husband. It was too soon for her to think about another. Too soon for him to be thinking of wanting her to think about him.

He played just the same, selfishly delighting in how she listened, seemingly enraptured with his playing. There was something, though, in how she looked at him. The concept caused him discomfort on many levels. Guilt over who she was—why he was there—assaulted his reason. Though it was selfish to think it might matter, the idea that he might never see her again after tomorrow prompted him. "May I speak freely, Mrs. Walters?"

"Please do."

He took a breath and leaned back on the porch swing. Unable to look her in the eye, he looked over her shoulder to the trees beyond, instead. "Your husband was a noble and great man."

"Yes, you have been kind to express numerous times, sir. It pleases me to know that you think…thought…so highly of him."

"About those letters, ma'am," he started.

"I would prefer you call me, Genevieve," she offered.

Zeke picked at a loose thread on his trouser knee. "Your husband, weary from days of battle, would often ask me to read them when the smoke and rigors of the day affected his eyes. He would lie on his cot. Your letters-- every word, I believe--is what sustained him, gave him hope and courage through many difficult times."

"I'm not sure whether to thank you or apologize that you had to read the pitiful, melancholy words of a new bride pining after her husband at war."

He looked at her then and smiled. "On the contrary. It was all I could do not to be envious of the man."

She placed her hand over her mouth and turned to leave.

Zeke touched her arm and she stilled. "Forgive me. I didn't intend to make you uncomfortable." He did not remove his hand. "To say that Captain

Walters was a lucky man is an understatement. What I--what any man would give to know such love, such longing as expressed in those letters is, forgive me, a priceless treasure.”

She looked at him then, face upturned in the pale moonlight. He could barely breathe. “Through those letters, I came to know the woman behind the words. Strong, yet compassionate. Giving. Kind. A woman able to endure solitude, yet give her soldier encouragement.”

“Please stop,” she whispered, then met his gaze. “I am not the noble woman you make me out to be. Far from it.”

“Even now you display your loyalty. And I admire you for that.”

His eyes locked with hers. Timidly, she lifted her hands to frame his face, and in the next instant her mouth met his. Passion. Fire and smoke. An aching desire followed. Each kiss opened the door a bit more to the forbidden. His hands circled her waist, drawing her close, his need evident. He’d fallen in love with her through her letters. Letters to her now dead husband. He felt her hand pressing on his heart, pushing him away. He took a step back, humiliated by his roguish behavior.

“My apologies, ma’am. I am overcome. I am deeply regretful for my actions and can only hope you can forgive the stolen kiss of a lonely soldier.”

He was barely able to look at her as he left in haste to return to his room. Before the sun rose, he’d left the clothes neatly folded on the bed and, donning his uniform, rode as far from Genevieve Walters as he could, fearing if he saw her again, he might never leave.

***

A knock on the door brought Zeke back to the present. At first the tapping was gentle, but with each subsequent knock they became louder, more determined. His gaze clung to the front door. As sure as the seasons change, he knew who stood on the other side of that door. The demons he’d wrestled with for over a dozen years had come to roost and he was about to face the first woman he’d ever given his heart to.

Chapter Thirteen

"Who's there?" a deep-throated voice boomed from within.

"It's Genevieve Walters. May I come in?

"I'm not having guests at present, Mrs. Walters."

She debated his answer, squared her shoulders, and knocked again. "I'm sorry Mr. Kinnison. This is a matter of utmost urgency."

A moment of silence ticked by.

"Suit yourself, but don't say I didn't warn you."

It was indeed possible that he was entertaining one of Madame's women. Not that a man and woman in bed was a sight she'd not seen before…or experienced. She quickly shoved away the thought.

Genevieve carefully opened the door, mentally preparing to accept whatever she encountered with decorum and dignity.

The sight before her wasn't at all what she'd expected. *Christian Kinnison.*

Her heart faltered as she looked across the room to where the rugged man sat soaking in a large copper tub by the fire. He had an old mirror propped on a table beside the tub and appeared to be finishing with shaving off his beard. His long, dark blond-brown hair lay plastered wet over his muscular shoulders. Mesmerized she watched a rivulet of water travel down his torso. An unexpected desire pulled at Genevieve. Embarrassed by her thoughts she forced herself to look away. "You didn't mention you were bathing, sir."

He chuckled and the sound of it sent shivers from the top of her head to the tips of her toes--stopping to awaken a few spots along the way.

"A moment ago, that fact didn't seem to matter, Mrs. Walters." He offered her a congenial smile. "Besides the best parts are covered. Now." He returned to his shaving. "What is it that you would ride clear out here alone to tell me?"

Finding her purpose, Genevieve held up the note, and yet again found herself taken aback with how the firelight shimmered on his handsome face, now almost void of hair. She'd forgotten the rugged jaw, his mouth with that tempting full lower lip, the dimple that formed when he smiled. *You had your chance, Genevieve. You pushed it away. This isn't about you or the past. It's about the present.* She blinked, pulling her thoughts in check. "It's from Penny, I'm afraid." *Did he even remember her? Was it possible the kiss meant far less to him than it had to her?*

He didn't look at her, but continued to inspect his work, studying his face in the small mirror. "Penny? She's run off, hasn't she?"

My heavens. She tried to quell the ache in her chest. He was a fine-looking man, still. Perhaps more so, given he had a bit of meat on his bones hewn to solid muscle from his mountain living. Those eyes—the stark blue of a mountain lake--stood out with a clarity that still took her breath away. The same eyes that now seemed to be looking directly into her soul.

"I don't want to say I told you so," he said.

His challenge jarred her fantasy. "Then don't." She shook her head. "I'm sorry things didn't work out for you, but that does not mean there isn't a right woman out there for you. I believe that every man needs a woman."

"You do? And why is that, Mrs. Walters?" He leaned back in the tub and held her gaze.

Flustered by his lack of concern about his state of undress, she attempted to rise to his challenge. "Well, Mr. Kinnison." She squared her shoulders. "It is our creed, our very purpose at the Benevolent Society of Lost Lambs to help create unions that will last."

"And how's that working for you, Mrs. Walters?" His voice lowered, causing tingles to skitter over her treacherous body. Tingles she hadn't had in places that had felt precious little in quite some time.

Which wasn't her purpose in being here, was it?

"I'm pleased to say that my success in procuring suitable matches here in Noelle has gone fairly well, if I do toot my own horn a bit."

He chuckled openly. "Be my guest. But, what about those that are not meant to be matched?" he asked. "Do you find that to be the case at times?"

He'd picked up a small glass with an amber liquid—whiskey, she'd be willing to bet. Suddenly, she pictured him in a chair reading by the fire. Drink at his side, those spectacles he wore from time to time perched on his handsome face. Had she just thought that? She darted him a quick look.

"You have an interesting way of looking at a man you've been trying to marry off to another woman," he said, curiosity seeming to edge into his voice.

"I'm quite certain I don't know what you mean," Genevieve replied with a sniff.

"What I mean is, I'd stake my life that you remember that kiss on the veranda as much as I do."

Lord above. She looked away, scrambling her wits. He *did* remember! "What kiss?" she attempted, albeit miserably, to be coy.

Truth be told, for years after she thought of it as one would hold tight to a blanket—every night—snuggling into the memory to keep her safe and secure. It was a woman's prerogative to cling to the familiar, wasn't it? Hadn't she just been made a widow? The protocol that she should be mourning over her dead husband caused her to push away a young soldier's affections—even as his honor and duty agreed. Hadn't he told her then how he'd fallen in love with her through the letters he'd been asked to read aloud to her husband? He'd been his confidant. The man he'd trusted with the most intimate details of his--and her--personal life.

In a moment of grief—weak from her recent loss and vulnerable— she'd kissed him. It was not a kiss shared between strangers. Rather, two hearts intimately knit together by admiration, respect, and yes, by common loss.

"I shall not lie to you," he said gruffly.

She met his steady gaze.

"I'm glad that Penny ran away," he said.

"What an awful thing to say about your intended," Genevieve admonished.

"Is it worse than to live a lie and be with someone you don't care for?"

She glanced away. "No, I suppose not."

"Or worse," he said quietly, "living without the one you truly care about?"

Genevieve's heart tumbled. She could not bring herself to look at the man. Fearful that he was validating what Penny had been able to see—what countless others in town might already suspect. She swallowed. "I think our focus should be on finding Penny."

"You mentioned that you received the note this morning. Why then, have you waited until midday to advise me on this matter?" he asked. "Penny must be nearly to the train by now."

Genevieve hesitated. Were she to answer directly, she'd be admitting something that only now was she beginning to resolve herself. What type of matchmaker would that make her? Would it be a betrayal to the pact she'd made with Penny, to the Society, and the pastor of Noelle? But had Penny really shown a willingness to try again at marriage, or was it simply

Genevieve's determined hope that she would?

"I suppose I was debating the situation," she said quietly. She lowered herself onto one of his table chairs. She'd folded and refolded Penny's note a number of times to the point the paper was tearing slightly. This was worse than any poker game she'd watched men play. She was carefully trying not to show her hand--what she still felt for him--at least, not before she knew his intentions.

"Debating what, precisely, Mrs. Walters?"

"Please," she said with a little more force than necessary. "It's Genevieve." She glanced at him then, softening her tone. "Please call me Genevieve. It's not as though we don't know each other."

He held her eyes with his captivating blue-eyed gaze. "Very well, Genevieve."

The softness in his tone caressed her every bit as though he'd touched her physically. Her body ached, remembering the pleasure, the passion between a man and a woman.

"Why are you here, Genevieve?"

There it was. She now had the choice to turn away—refuse this fragile second chance of something she didn't fully understand. For months, she'd been tutoring others on this very thing—encouraging them to take a leap of faith, embrace a new beginning. But was she able to heed her own advice? Life out here was far different, far more uncertain, more dangerous than New York or Denver.

"Why don't you read me Penny's note?" he asked.

She studied his challenging gaze, aware that if the circumstances were different—if she were more brazen like Madame Bonheur or the other girls at La Maison des Chats--she might well be climbing into that tub with him at this very moment. She was no virgin. Still, her face heated madly from her thoughts.

"Is that pretty blush on my account, or from the content of the note? Either way, I am intrigued," he said, his mouth curling wickedly at one corner.

Genevieve took a cleansing breath and began to read Penny's note aloud, careful to be as clear and concise in the process, even though her skin seemed to be on fire. "*We can correspond once I'm settled. I shall look forward to hearing more about this man you believe represents the best possible husband. If he is as wonderful as you say he is...*" Genevieve cleared her throat, the truth buckling her ability to speak clearly. She moistened her lips, unable to look at Zeke. *"Then perhaps you should consider him for yourself,"* she finished reading.

A soft chuckle brought her eyes to his. "You debated coming here because you weren't certain if what Penny said was true, or if I might feel similarly?"

Genevieve straightened, plucking an imaginary thread from her skirt. After all, she was a woman—a woman with needs. Not unlike a man. She lifted one shoulder slightly. "I suppose the possibility has since crossed my mind," she said, hoping the lilt in her voice didn't give away her uncertainty. "Nonetheless, how was I to know you even remembered me?" But he saw right through her façade, offering a sexy, toe-curling smile.

"I'd like to offer you a deal," he said.

"A deal, Mr. Kinnison?"

"I want to hear you call me, Zeke." He raised a brow.

She found it a strange bargaining chip, but complied. "Very well, Zeke."

His grin widened. "That, Genevieve, was not the deal. But I do admire the sound of my name on your tongue."

Tingles. So many tingles.

"My deal is this," he said. "Stay with me this afternoon and allow me to address—at least—some of your concerns."

Desire heated Genevieve's blood. He hadn't proposed anything of a carnal nature, of course. But what else could a naked man in a tub mean by such a proposal?

"If, by some chance, you decide that your coming here was a mistake, then we shall part amiably. Agreed?"

"Oh," she said with a demur smile. "You're not that kind of man, Mr. Kinnison. You deserve better."

"Indeed, Genevieve. And I'm determined to convince you in every way possible that I have found the very best woman I could ever hope for. I want you, dear woman, to be my partner, my wife, my lover—my friend." He held her gaze and held out his hand. "And with any luck, you'll take off those pretty shoes, take my hand, and let me convince you."

A joyous freedom bubbled inside her. She leaned down, unlacing her boots with quick dexterity and pulled them off, setting them carefully next to his by the front door. A sense of belonging, of being safe—being loved—

settled over her. She'd not thought her heart could ever feel this way—so alive, so full of promise—again.

She stood and walked to the edge of the tub and put her hand in his. "I may need help with my dress." With a rumbling laugh, he tugged her into the tub, freeing the shackles she'd placed around her heart.

"That, my love, will not be a problem." He cupped her cheek, his calloused fingers brushing over her skin. He leaned forward and kissed her with a tender reverence. Years of pushing away memories melted as his kisses deepened, becoming more insistent. Every nerve in her body awoke to the luxurious sensation of being held in his arms.

"You've no idea how many nights I lay awake thinking of you like this." He pulled back, holding her gaze as his fingers caressed her cheek, trailing down the front of her throat to the top buttons of her bodice. He unfastened each, exposing her skin above her underpinnings. "I've imagined how soft your skin is, how it would taste against my mouth."

His gentle seduction encouraged her to place her hand over his and guide him to the swell just above her corset. She smoothed her hand over his bare shoulder, relishing the sinewy muscle bunching, moving beneath her fingers. Lost in the euphoric bliss of his heated kisses, the taste of whiskey on his tongue, the all-male scent of him—she squealed when he stood and lifted her in his arms. Her sodden clothes left a watery trail across the floor. He gently dropped her to her feet by the bed.

"You'll be warmer out of those clothes, Genevieve. I promise."

He didn't have to ask her twice.

Chapter Fourteen

Zeke watched her sleep for the better part of an hour. Even in the throes of passion that afternoon, he'd seen the dark circles beneath her beautiful eyes, wishing he could take away her worry about the railroad agreement and her part in it.

He sat on the edge of the bed and picked up the watch fob that had belonged to his Captain. Zeke felt a familiar guilt breeze over his heart. He had still a great deal of respect for his captain—his friend—even this long after his death. But his heart wholly as loyally to the precious woman lying asleep in his bed.

"He chose you, I think." He felt her gentle hand on his back. He shifted to look at her, astounded by the grace he'd been given of Providence bringing her to him again after all these years.

"Chose me?" Zeke asked. His heart was full, yet his good fortune warred with his guilt.

"You told me once that you fell in love with me through my letters to Levi," she said looking up at him, her dark hair spilling over her pale shoulders.

"God help me, I did. But I never wanted…never thought--" He looked away unable to finish.

"Never thought that you'd have to follow through on the promise you had made? Levi may have been a great captain, but I think he knew his love for me was not the kind he saw on your face as you read my letters to him."

Zeke caught her gaze. "How could he know?"

She smiled softly. "Because, my love, I see how you look at me. Even now as you did the first time we met."

"I cannot deny what I felt then, or now." Zeke was afraid to allow his good fortune to last, however. Her life was in Denver. What had changed in the last few hours was knowing he belonged in her arms, but not knowing whether to stay in Noelle or go with her to Denver.

Zeke smiled. She hadn't flinched, hadn't run when his scars came into view in the flickering lamplight. Quite the opposite--she traced each one, followed by a tender kiss, the gesture alone earning another hour of bliss in her arms.

"You realize you snore," he said, lifting an errant lock of hair from her face.

"You're fibbing." Her eyes widened, her cheeks blushing faintly.

He grinned. "I swear it's true. Thought you might wake the dead."

She batted his arm, but smiled all the same.

It wasn't a topic he wanted to broach, but it was better to know now the lay of the land. Had this been an afternoon of pure bliss simply been intended to make up for some missed opportunity years before?

"You're thinking," she said, eyeing him. "About what?"

He searched her eyes. "Us, I guess. What's to happen now?"

She pulled the blanket up around her as she sat up. "That depends, I suppose," she said.

"Depends?"

"On how we feel?" She shrugged, her smile accentuating her well-kissed lips. Mischief sparkled in her dark eyes. Just looking at her made him want to forget the realities of the world outside and take her back into his arms. He shifted and cleared his throat. They needed to talk. Their future depended on it.

"I think you know how I feel, Genevieve. I've been very clear on my position. And at present, there is nothing that appeals to me more than showing you once again what you mean to me. How I long to make you happy…if you'll have me. But I cannot ask you to give up your life's work in Denver."

"Well, that's a fine how-do-you-do. I'll have you know, Mr. Kinnison, that I am not one of those saloon girls you can bed and walk away from without another thought."

Zeke listened carefully, his heart hoping he'd heard what she was trying to say. "I do not see you in that way, Genevieve," he said calmly. This odd banter was not helping his decision to not touch her again until this matter was settled.

"A good man, a decent man would offer a proposal of marriage," she offered with a raised brow.

Zeke's heart nearly flew from his chest. "I would be honored if you would marry me, Genevieve. And I don't care if we live in Denver, Noelle--anywhere you wish. As long as we're together--that's all that matters to me." He leaned over and kissed her softly. "Say you'll marry me." He leaned back to search her beautiful eyes. "Tonight."

A smile brightened her face. She hugged his neck. "Yes, of course. We can get married and then there will be only one position left to fill."

Zeke grinned and raised his brow.

"You are incorrigible, Mr. Kinnison," she smiled, brushing her hands through his hair.

He lowered his mouth to hers. There was much to get resolved. Where would they live? What might become of Noelle? How would he force himself to leave this bed, stand before a crowd to speak his vows, and not be thinking of getting her right back here the whole time?

***

Zeke guided Buttercup and Blue hitched to his wagon sleigh down the darkening trail. Twin oil lamps swayed on the posts providing a bit of light to their path.

There was no question she wanted to marry him. No question he wanted to marry her. She reached beneath the lap blanket and rested her hand on his knee.

"Be careful, Genevieve. Or I'll not be able to properly present myself before Pastor Hammond." He gave her a lop-sided grin.

She moved her hand away and he grabbed it bringing it to his lips for a gentle kiss. "Have you considered how your family in Denver will respond to our marriage?"

She smiled and rested her cheek on his shoulder. "I doubt you remember how quite taken my mother-in-law was with you, sir. You were truly a calm in her world at a most difficult time. She will be thrilled. However…" She paused and they rode a moment or two in silence.

Zeke felt the smack of a brisk cold wind on his freshly shaven face. He knew by the scent in the air that a snow storm would be arriving within days. They would need to make a decision quickly of when to leave if they wanted to reach the train before snow made travel through the mountain pass dangerous.

"What if we were to stay here in Noelle?" She seemed far away in her thoughts. "Of course, with Penny on her way now to Denver that would resolve the mission needing to find another director. I could simply write them a note offering my full recommendation of her." Her sigh held a note of resignation. "I only wish I'd been able to speak with her before she left."

Puzzled that she'd want to stay in the barely civilized town, he took her hand in his. "Are you certain this is what you want, Genevieve?"

She straightened and pinned him with a determined look. "Do you feel I'm not suited to live in Noelle?"

"Of course not. It's just that I thought you might miss all the fine houses, the shops, and afternoon teas."

"Christian Ezekiel, my life's work has been in a mission funded by a church organization. The finer things in life are nice, I suppose. But there are things far greater and much more satisfying." She smiled up at him, her face aglow in the moonlight coming over the ridge.

He grinned. "Woman, I do like the way you think."

"You'll always know what I'm thinking." She held his gaze. "Quite possibly if you want to hear it or not." She nudged his shoulder.

"It's one of the things I admire about you, Genevieve. That and I confess I'm brought to my knees every time you say my name." He pulled on the reins and brought the wagon to a stop. They sat in front of the Golden Nugget.

"The wagon has stopped," she said, her eyes locked with his.

"That's because I wish to kiss you." He leaned forward.

She averted his advance with an ornery grin. "After we're married, Mr. Kinnison." She glanced at the crowd gathered outside the Nugget saloon. "We're here to ask Pastor Hammond to marry us. Why, folks might get the wrong idea were they to see us kiss in public."

"I suspect" --he leaned down to whisper in her ear--"they are curious about who is getting married tonight."

Zeke hopped down from the wagon and heard the whispered comments about his clean-shaven face. He lifted Genevieve to her feet and offered his arm. Amid inquisitive looks the onlookers parted as they entered the saloon.

Inside, Woody, Jack, and Pastor Hammond were busy arranging the chairs into short, neat rows.

"Well, Pastor Hammond, you can't say we didn't do our best," Woody said aloud. "Noelle has seen ten marriages in the past few days. That's something we can be proud of. Surely the railroad would allow us to compromise a bit?"

Molly Thornton with her precious goose tucked beneath the arm of her new husband, Storm followed Zeke and Genevieve into the room and took seats close to the door.

"He will make a wonderful father," Genevieve whispered to Zeke looking at Storm and the goose.

"Mrs. Walters." Pastor Hammond walked to her, his hand extended to take hers. "Culver has already explained everything."

Zeke looked around the room and realized Nacho and Fina; Woody and his wife, Meizhen; Jack's wife, Birdie; and Jack's grandfather, Gus, were already seated. Even Sherriff Draven, looking a lot less sour than usual, was there with Pearl.

"Do you have any idea what's going on?" Zeke leaned down to whisper in Genevieve's ear.

She shook her head. "Good evening Pastor Hammond. I'm so sorry about Penelope."

Pastor Hammond offered Zeke a smile. "Yes, I can see the groom-to-be is terribly distraught."

The door opened and Liam Fulton and his bride, Avis, walked in. Following close behind was Doc Deane and his new bride, Cara, as well as Minnie and her husband, Hugh Montgomery.

"Pastor Hammond," Genevieve said. "If you'll excuse me a moment, I need to return this to Birdie. But I believe Mr. Kinnison needs a word with you."

"But I thought we were going to ask him together--" Zeke glanced from Genevieve's departing form to the preacher's expectant face.

"Something you wish to ask, son?" Pastor Hammond offered a congenial smile.

Zeke suddenly had difficulty finding his tongue. "Well, sir. I realize this may seem a bit unorthodox from what was planned…it's well…just that…."

Culver Daniels appeared at Zeke's side.

"It's just that he'd like to request you to marry him and Mrs. Walters." His large hand landed on Zeke's shoulder. "Ain't that right, Zeke?"

Pastor Hammond looked at Zeke. "Well now, are those *your* wishes, son?"

Genevieve returned. Her face was aglow. Placed over her face, she wore the veil Birdie had made. In her hand she carried a small bouquet of juniper branches, tied with a gingham ribbon.

"What I'm trying to say, Pastor Hammond, is that by some miracle our lives have managed to come together again after all this time and--" Zeke seemed to suddenly stumble over his words, the realization of his dream coming true hit him.

Pastor Hammond reached in his pocket, searching for his watch.

"Blast it all, where is that watch?" He mumbled, busy with searching his pockets for the lost article. "Please go on. I'm riveted, truly."

Zeke scratched his chin. "As it happens, wouldn't it satisfy one of the obligations required by the railroad if Genevieve and I to marry? *Not* that I feel any obligation, of course…"

"Of course, it's because you love her." Pastor Hammond squinted into his vest pocket.

Hearing it said out loud by another brought a warmth to his heart. Zeke grinned. "Yessir. It would be my profound honor and privilege to spend the rest of my days seeking to create a happy life with her." He placed his arm around Genevieve. It was the most open he'd been about his feelings in years.

"Awwww," arose a chorus of responses from the ladies present. Even a few of the men seemed to soften at Zeke's heartfelt admission.

"I can't think of a better reason than that, son." preacher said. "I can't see why it wouldn't work. Of course, the final decision would rest with Percival and his uncle." Pastor Hammond glanced up and smiled at the pinched-faced man, who stood with arms folded at the back of the saloon.

Percival crossed his skinny arms over his chest. "He didn't draw a straw."

Pastor Hammond tossed a grimace at the persnickety man. "We've had brides and groom changing places all week long, Percival. What's the difference of one more?" The preacher looked to be exhausted. Zeke couldn't blame him.

"The woman lives in Denver."

All eyes turned to Genevieve.

Genevieve scanned their faces. "That is…was true." She looked at the preacher. "May I explain?"

He nodded. "Of course."

The pride on Genevieve's face was unmistakable as she glanced around the room at each of the new brides. "Denver has nothing on the beauty and warmth of Noelle. And each of you has shown me an enterprising resilience and determination that is needed to make a community thrive. We'll need women like you to teach our schools--"

"Schools?" Woody interjected. "When did we get a school?"

Pastor gave him a droll smile. "We haven't yet, Woody. Go on, Mrs. Walters."

"And we'll need good midwives when the children start coming." Genevieve smiled, looking at the women gathered there.

Pastor Hammond cleared his throat. "Yes, well it appears Noelle is going to be a busy place. Maybe we should get on with the marriage part before we start talking about children?"

Keiza's little Jemimah wailed loudly as if on cue, causing a titter of laughter to ripple throughout the room.

Genevieve smiled. "What I'm trying to say is I think Noelle is a perfect place to bring ladies who are seeking new adventures in business and matrimony in the new west." She looked at the preacher. "Once the railroad is established, Noelle is sure to thrive, and I would like to stay right here and be a part of that, along with the rest of you."

She looked up at Zeke. In her eyes, he saw his future. Noelle's future. "If life has taught me nothing else, Pastor Hammond, it's made me a believer in possibility, in new beginnings—in second chances," she said.

"That's good enough for me!" Pastor Hammond clamped his hand over Zeke's, clasping it together with Genevieve's.

"If you're ready?" He looked from one to another, then ushered them to the front of the seated group.

Birdie, who'd stayed at the front to adjust the veil, spoke softly to Genevieve. "It's too bad there's nothing to place on the tree with all the other lovely ornaments."

Agatha Boonesbury stood from where she'd been sitting behind Gus Peregrine. "I believe Gus has something he could offer for the tree."

Gus, his bushy brows knit over his amber-colored eyes, peered at Agatha. "I do believe yer misguided, madam."

She narrowed her gaze. "Now Gus-Gus." Agatha smiled at him. "Are you certain? Why, what's that lovely gold chain dangling from your coat pocket."

He pulled out the watch fob. "I found this out front," Gus sputtered. "Laying on the walk. Fell clean between the cracks."

"There's my watch!" Pastor Hammond walked over to Gus. "It was my father's. Thank you, Gus." Taking his place in front of Zeke and Genevieve, Pastor Hammond smiled.

"Dearly beloved--"

"Pastor Hammond?" Zeke interrupted. "I have a gift for my bride. If I may?" Pastor Hammond checked his watch, cast a tolerant look to the ceiling, and nodded with a tolerant smile.

Zeke pulled out his harmonica and holding Genevieve's gaze, played her the tune he played the night they had first kissed. When he finished she held out her hand, took the small red mouth pipe and carefully tucked it on the tree branches alongside the other ornaments—one for each of the wedded couples that had been mysteriously placed on the tree over the past few days.

Returning to Zeke, she placed her hands in his and together they faced Pastor Hammond.

"Dearly beloved, we are gathered here…"